PRAISE FOR THI

"This book takes a very practical and useful approach to the popular topic of "resiliency." The authors use vignettes to describe the experience of women faced with career challenges – and provide tools, templates, practices, and practical links to help readers move from declining to surviving and finally to thriving in their workplace. They are clear about the challenges that still face women at work, but are optimistic about ways that they can overcome barriers and become architects of their destiny through pursuing their well-developed strategies. A great resource for women, it can also inform their managers, mentors, partners, and colleagues about ways to create larger opportunities that can benefit individual women and enrich organizations."

B. KIM BARNES, CEO, Barnes & Conti Associates, Inc., Author, *Exercising Influence: Making Things Happen at Work, at Home, and In Your Community*

"Strength, power, and resiliency are the keys to not just surviving but to thriving in societies often designed to limit women. This book and the lessons learned will help you to unlock your natural, basic instinct to survive, cope and conquer challenging situations; whether they be personal, professional or domestic."

CJ BOWRY, Founder, Sal's Shoes

"*Shift Into Thrive* organizes three important concepts into six pragmatic strategies that female professionals can, and have, employed successfully. First, female professionals have more choice than they may imagine, second, having a growth mindset is essential, and third, women can do the strategy thing. This is an important read for every woman who has ever struggled or felt a lack of support along her professional journey. Everyone who reads the book will walk away with one key message, 'Thriving is a choice.'"

MICHELLE BRAILSFORD, Head of European Division, Jupiter Consulting Group, Member of the PWN-London Advisory Board

"This book provides strategies and activities that enable you to move forward from your diagnosis and to thrive rather than simply survive. There is an emphasis on strengths and the importance of your network for professional accomplishment, whether to obtain support in challenging moments or to develop one's career, a subject which is very dear to me. I encourage all women, as well as men, to read this book to find the keys to success."

FRÉDÉRIQUE CINTRAT, Founding President, AXIELLES.COM,
Author, *Comment l'ambition vient aux filles?*

"Resiliency is an area that any woman must have in her tool box to thrive in the professional world. This book succinctly defines the six components that comprise resiliency into concrete, understandable terms. The strategies and action planning to strengthen one's resiliency are clear, thorough and attainable. Once the reader completes these steps, they will not only have the key to success in their professional life but also in their personal life as the authors have embraced the essence of how strong resiliency leads to personal and professional growth."

KAREN FAULIS, CEO, Hi-Desert Medical Center

"*Shift Into Thrive* translates sound research into actionable strategies to help women succeed at work, without losing themselves. Clear case studies, practical action plans, and useful resources support each of the resiliency strategies outlined, and help readers put the ideas into practice with confidence. Women, managers, organizations, and educational institutions will all find this book helpful as we collectively work to unlock the full capability of our entire workforce. Lynn Schmidt and Kevin Nourse have delivered a tour de force!"

ALEXIS A. FINK, PhD, General Manager, Talent Intelligence &
Analytics, Intel Corporation

"*Shift Into Thrive* requires courage to unlock the Six Strategies that unleash the power to change lives—our own and our fellow travelers' on the shared leadership journey. This is an indispensable handbook for leaders of the future."

FRANCES HESSELBEIN, The Frances Hesselbein Leadership Institute

"This exciting book by Drs. Lynn Schmidt and Kevin Nourse provides unique and practical insights into personal resiliency. Using a tightly woven combination of personal stories, action steps, and excellent worksheets, the book provides an actionable framework for women who wish to achieve more success in their careers. While working women are the primary target audience, the resiliency insights apply to varied audiences, including organizational leaders. As a leadership coach, I appreciate the self-coaching approach used in this timely book."

PAT MATHEWS, MCC, President, Mathews Associates,
Founding Faculty, Institute for Transformational Leadership,
Georgetown University

"*Shift Into Thrive* is not only a fantastic read for working women but a source of great information and ideas for all leaders. In fact, I think men, in particular, will benefit by understanding how to better support the women in their lives and understand the unique challenges they encounter on their career journey."

KEVIN OAKES, CEO, i4cp (Institute for Corporate Productivity)

"All too often women fail to prevail when times get tough, such as when inequities exist, or others attempt to derail their progress. Rather than bounce back after an unpleasant experience, they give up, only to miss the opportunity to contribute to their fullest. Lynn Schmidt and Kevin Nourse have developed a book that enables women in all professions and walks of life to come back even stronger when setbacks occur. By implementing the six strategies outlined in this book, you can take the action necessary to unleash the resiliency inherent in you and power through to reach your full potential."

PATTI PHILLIPS, PhD, Co-founder, President & CEO,
ROI Institute, Inc.

"The Professional Women's Network (PWN) Global believes that resilience is a key competence that helps us grow our potential. We are constantly learning to cope with the multi-faceted aspects of our family, professional and societal roles. With women often carrying most of the burden at home, besides focusing on building their professional careers, we are eager for our PWN community and beyond to learn about the six resilience-building strategies. With the right approach, women will be supported to feel more in control of their lives and their reactions to everyday situations. A great book if you are looking to advance professionally."

SONYA RICHARDSON, PWN Global President

"In the growing panoply of leadership and management writings, this book stands out. Guided by a solid understanding of the latest research, the action steps and tools offered are concrete and eminently practical. Resilience is a factor long noted as an important ingredient to success yet not well understood by leaders. Combining an understanding of resilience specifically for women has created an engaging and compelling book that acknowledges the particular issues that women face in the workplace and their consulting practices. Schmidt and Nourse have achieved that rare goal of a well-written work that you will read, take action on, and remember for years to come."

KATRINA S. ROGERS, PhD, President, Fielding Graduate University

"I just finished your book earlier today, and wow, what an amazing read! It resonated with me on so many levels; taking me back to various stages of my career where I have been in a state of decline, survive or thrive. I appreciate the real-life case studies and the plethora of useful and practical resource materials. The book is a critical guide for all women to reset, refresh, or remind themselves to examine the health of their careers. I will never underestimate the value of continually building and nurturing my support network."

CHRISTINE SCAPPA, Senior Vice President, Sage

"What a fresh and incisive analysis of those factors that ultimately enable any of us to manage and navigate the peaks and valleys of our career. Whether you're a woman, a man, a young professional or a grizzled veteran, there are insights that you can gain through reading and re-

reading this book that will enable you to understand how to craft a personalized strategy that creates the resilience and resolve necessary to cope and ultimately succeed in any organizational setting!"

TERRY D. SIMONETTE, President & CEO, Capital Impact Partners

"The theoretical claims in *Shift Into Thrive* are immediately underlined by real life examples and numerous easily applicable tools from situational assessments to actionable exercises with the invitation to do them. And if you do, you can't help but succeed in your professional and personal life. The tools enable the readers to see themselves in relationship to the bigger picture and to understand what is the most natural and logical next steps in their journeys to move in a meaningful direction and sustain the motivation and energy throughout the process."

LEDA TURAI-PETRAUSKIENE, MA, MSc, MCC,
Leadership Development Partner, Executive and Leadership Team Coach

"Development specifically designed for women leaders has become a fast-growing subset of the executive coaching profession. This book demonstrates why: Women face vastly different challenges in the workplace than their male counterparts. Drs. Schmidt and Nourse provide many strategies, examples and actionable steps to help women thrive. Compelling first-person stories from women bring it all to life. A book useful not just for women, but their bosses, organizations and the men who support them!"

BRIAN O. UNDERHILL, PhD, Founder & CEO, CoachSource, LLC,
Author, *Executive Coaching for Results*

"Resiliency is a must have to be a sustainable, long lasting, and successful leader. Resiliency is critical to achieving long-term goals for both companies and individuals. In *Shift Into Thrive* Lynn and Kevin describe how to build your resiliency and thrive, tips included."

DOMENICO ZACCONE, Trusted Advisor @ DPZ&Partners and
Executive Chairman of Gold Plast Group

SHIFT INTO THRIVE

SIX
STRATEGIES
FOR WOMEN
TO UNLOCK
THE POWER
OF RESILIENCY

LYNN SCHMIDT PHD
KEVIN NOURSE PHD

Bobo Publishing
1321 Fairmont Street, NW Suite 307
Washington, DC 20009
202-462-6252

Printed in the United States of America

ISBN (Paperback): 978-0-9975641-0-5
ISBN (E-Book): 978-0-9975641-1-2

Library of Congress Control Number: 2016907883

Cover and Interior Design by INKSPIRAL DESIGN
www.inkspiraldesign.com

To OUR MOTHERS, Maggie Nourse and Erma Schmidt.
You bravely faced and resiliently navigated adversity, from which
we draw inspiration for our lives and work.

CONTENTS

AUTHORS' NOTE

We wrote this book to enable women to thrive in the workplace and experience an extraordinary career journey accompanied by growth, success, and satisfaction. We believe the world would be a better place if women achieved greater equality in the workforce. This book focuses on six powerful resiliency strategies that women have used successfully to thrive and grow in the face of workplace challenges. This book has been many years in the making, drawing on individual and collective sources about resiliency during its development. We grew up in families where our grandmothers, mothers, sisters, and aunts told stories about the difficulties they experienced navigating their work lives. Those stories made a strong impression on us. These women brought exceptional talents to the workplace, yet faced ongoing struggles to achieve satisfaction. To thrive and grow at work wasn't often considered an option.

Rarely is authoring a book a solitary endeavor. We conducted interviews and participated in informal discussions with over 100 executive coaches and women around the world. On a very personal level, our own experiences navigating career challenges within organizations gave us a deep sense of admiration and respect for women facing similar situations. As executive coaches and human resource professionals, we have heard firsthand accounts of dozens of women who have thrived in the face of career challenges and derailment. During our dissertation research on career derailment and resiliency we read hundreds of books, scholarly articles, and blog posts. We spoke with other experts and attended professional conferences. This book incorporates insights gained from many of these resources.

A major source of insights included in this book came from recent original research we conducted. We began by interviewing nearly two dozen executive coaches who worked with women leaders experiencing career derailment. These coaches shared the strategies they used to help their clients thrive despite their clients' painful experiences. We then interviewed a number of women leaders to understand their experiences of potential or actual career derailment and their resiliency process. Subsequently, we sent an electronic survey to several hundred executive coaches to confirm the themes and strategies we uncovered in the earlier interviews with executive coaches and women leaders.

We adapted the resiliency strategy stories in this book to eliminate identifying details and to ensure the anonymity of the individuals we interviewed. In many cases, we have combined the information from multiple interviews to present a compilation of experiences that highlight the concepts. We modified quotes used for clarity, and to maintain the anonymity of the interviewees. Finally, we included personal stories in this book written by women who have experienced significant career challenges and thrived, not just survived. Their personal accounts of navigating adversity are inspiring and motivating.

This book has four audiences that will benefit from the content. The primary target audience is working women around the world, including those who are entrepreneurs, individual contributors, and leaders. We structured the book to include practical action steps women can proactively take to avoid or minimize the adverse impact of career challenges. The resiliency strategies apply to both small and large challenges. By applying these strategies, women can increase their ability to thrive in their careers and their personal lives.

A second target audience that will benefit from this book is people developers, including human resource, talent management, career development, and coaching professionals. This book is a significant resource to help these experts gain insights into the experiences of women facing career challenges, and the resiliency strategies that will help them thrive. People developers can use these strategies as they work with their clients, providing the book as a resource.

The third audience that will benefit from this book is organizational leaders. Organizational leaders, through their organizations, play a key role in helping women build the resiliency necessary to overcome work challenges. By implementing actions that eliminate roadblocks and help women build resiliency, organizations will be able to make more effective use of diverse talent, retain female employees, and increase business results. Organizational leaders at coaching schools and universities can incorporate this book into their teaching curricula.

A fourth audience is men, as male readers will benefit from this book as well. By understanding the experiences that women have in the workforce, men can provide support to the women they live and work with. While much of our research focused on the experiences of women and the unique ways that they experience career challenges, these six resiliency strategies are useful to anyone, male or female.

The ability to maintain one's resiliency and thrive in the midst of adversity is not a given. Rather, it is an intentional choice. When individuals consciously make that choice, they are better equipped to not just survive, but to thrive, and to be transformed by career challenges. Building resiliency can enable women around the world to create the extraordinary careers that they desire and deserve.

ONE

NAVIGATING CAREER ADVERSITY: CHOOSING TO THRIVE

Everything can be taken from a man but one thing: the last of human freedoms—to choose one's attitude in any given set of circumstances, to choose one's own way.
— VIKTOR FRANKL

She had every reason to give up, given the substantial challenges and setbacks she faced in her life and career. However, Oprah Winfrey made a conscious choice to grow, and as a result, she thrived. She experienced some setbacks in her career as a news anchor that could have easily caused her to give up. While anchoring for WJZ-TV in Baltimore, Oprah was demoted to a lower-level position in 1977. Colleagues at the TV station described how ineffective she was in reporting the news, especially in contrast with her highly polished veteran co-anchor. Several months later, Oprah reluctantly accepted a role as cohost of a talk show, even though she did not believe that she would be accepted as a legitimate journalist.

She excelled in the talk show format, eventually leading the show to national syndication and beating Phil Donahue in the ratings. Oprah explained, "Anything can be a miracle, a blessing, an opportunity if you choose to see it that way. Had I not been demoted from my six o'clock anchor position in Baltimore back in 1977, the talk show gig would have never happened when it did." In a 2012 interview with her, talk show host

David Letterman noted, "Most people would use this life as an excuse. You were not consumed; you prevailed."

Oprah Winfrey's journey to success and her optimistic attitude toward adversity embodies resiliency and provides a robust foundation for this book. In this chapter, you will be introduced to the nature of career adversity for women, the importance of resiliency, and the Resiliency Framework. You will also gain insights on how best to use this book and specific chapters that may be most relevant for the unique challenges you face in establishing or rebuilding your resiliency.

WOMEN AREN'T THRIVING

Women are not yet thriving in the workforce. They often earn less than men for the same roles, don't receive promotions as frequently, and experience gender inequalities that men don't experience. According to an analysis of data from the World Economic Forum's Human Capital Report by Mercer, women are underrepresented in the workforce in every country and for every age group. At the same time, the available talent pool of females in the workforce continues to grow, as more than 50 percent of college graduates are now women. Even though the number of highly educated and skilled women is growing, women hold less than a quarter of senior management positions globally. Frustrated, women are leaving the traditional workforce in increasing numbers and becoming entrepreneurs. Unfortunately, becoming an entrepreneur doesn't eliminate the gender inequities. In a 2015 study presented in the Kauffman Policy Digest, researchers found that women are 50 percent less likely to start their own business compared to men. Women experience incredible challenges daily as members of the workforce. The challenges require that women have an ability to build resiliency so they can thrive, not just survive, in today's working world. Women need to be resilient to be successful in their professions and achieve the career satisfaction they deserve.

Women bring some unique and valuable perspectives to the workforce.

Gender diversity in the workforce allows businesses to establish a competitive advantage, and many statistics show that companies with a diverse workforce outperform other companies. For-profit organizations that embrace gender diversity have been shown to be more profitable. One McKinsey study found that gender-diverse companies were fifteen percent more likely to outperform the median performance measures of their industry. The *Financial Times* reported on a study conducted in Sweden that found greater numbers of female board members translated to higher sales and stock returns. Another McKinsey study suggests that improving equality for women in organizations could have a twelve trillion dollar positive impact globally. As noted in the Mercer report, progress for women in the workforce is slow despite the passage of equal-pay legislation and greater global awareness about the barriers women face, leading these researchers to conclude it could be several decades before gender equality is reached. Even worse, researchers at the World Economic Forum suggest that the gap between men and women's wages will take over 100 years to close at the current pace. Other statistics underscore the continued struggle for women in the working world:

- Findings from Bain & Company's five-year research project on gender parity suggest that after two years in the workplace, women's aspirations dropped 60 percent and their confidence 50 percent. The study concluded that the current work environment does not provide women with female role models or organizational support. The workplace endorses an ideal worker stereotype that doesn't resonate with most women.

- The U.S. Department of Labor recently found that white women earn only 75 cents for every dollar earned by white men. These findings are even worse for African American women (65 cents compared to white men) and Hispanic women (55 cents for every dollar earned by white men).

- A United Nations delegation of human rights experts evaluated gender equality and determined that women have "missing rights." The U.S. is one of three countries in the world that does not guarantee women paid maternity leave, impacting women's ability to contribute financially to the families that depend on them.

- McKinsey & Company, based on a 2012 survey of 60 major U.S. corporations, notes that while 53 percent of entry-level employees are female, only 19 percent of C-level executives are women.

- The United Nations conducted a study and found that while the number of women in senior governmental roles has doubled since 1995, women account for only 22 percent of members in legislative bodies around the world.

- According to recent figures from the Pew Research Center, women accounted for only 16.9 percent of Fortune 500 board positions in 2013 compared to 9.6 percent in 1995, and only 5.2 percent of Fortune 50 CEO positions in 2014 compared to none in 1995.

- A 2014 Catalyst study found women hold only 20.8 percent of the board seats at Canadian stock index companies. A range of 3.1 percent (Japan) to 19.2 percent (Australia) of Asia-Pacific stock index company board seats were occupied by women. Even among forward-thinking northern European countries, the best performing country was Norway, with only 35.5 percent of board seats being occupied by women.

What accounts for these poor statistics and the pervasive lack of progress for women's equality in the workplace? Among the most substantial causes are societal and organizational barriers, including deeply ingrained gender stereotypes and discriminatory practices. Another cause is the lack of sufficient support systems and programs to help women navigate the journey. Gender stereotypes play a substantive role in blocking the career success of women because they can lead to discriminatory practices in hiring, development, promotion, compensation, and evaluation in the organization. For example, according to the U.S. Department of Labor, "About 40 percent of that pay gap can't be explained by differences in experiences, skills, or the jobs held by men and women. It appears to be largely the product of stubborn discrimination." Researcher Madeline Heilman notes how stereotypes are translated into "consequences for hiring, starting salary and job placement decisions, as well as opportunities for skill development, pay raises, and promotions."

Stereotypes often have the most negative impact on performance expectations, particularly for professions that are traditionally male dominated, such as organizational leadership roles. A common stereotypical view suggests that men take charge of things and women take care of others. Therefore, a woman would not possess the skills needed to succeed in leadership roles. People commonly assume that the qualities of an effective leader, also known as implicit theories of leadership, are masculine. According to the Pew Research Center, more than 40 percent of respondents in a study believed that organizations are just not ready to hire women leaders or promote them to senior ranks. *Harvard Business Review* cited a study where college students were asked to evaluate two job applicants with similar qualifications. The researchers then revealed that one of the applicants was a working mother. The college students in the study assigned working mothers less compensation than childless women. Parenting status did not affect male candidates.

Career adversity consists of unforeseen challenges people encounter in their professions as a result of factors they can control as well as those triggered by societal and organizational context, which they can't control. These challenges come in different forms, from relatively minor issues to significant barriers. If these adverse situations are not managed appropriately, they can escalate to the point of causing derailment. Career derailment occurs when an individual is hired for a role and is expected to be successful, but is subsequently perceived as incapable of performing that role. The individual may then be demoted, fired, asked to resign, or forced out. This situation is surprisingly common, with some researchers estimating that 50 percent of managers face derailment. Career derailment is costly both for those who experience it and for organizations. Adverse impacts include the costs of recruiting and hiring replacements, and the impact on productivity.

Researchers have developed models identifying the sources of career derailment affecting both men and women. One framework noted four sources of derailment affecting women leaders:

- Personal factors such as the woman's leadership style, deficiencies in a support network, relationship with the boss, and an inability to achieve business objectives.

- Other individuals' perceptions, including sabotage by others in the organization, new senior leadership, or the negative reactions of others to a competent woman.

- Organizational factors, including discontinued business operations.

- Societal issues, including overt or covert discrimination in the workplace, and gender bias.

While many of these sources of derailment are common to both genders, women are more likely to be affected by discrimination and personal factors. For example, women who exhibit behavior typically associated with men, such as directly asking for a raise, often acquire negative reputations and may become marginalized. Also, some women are held to higher performance standards than their male peers and are promoted into strategic leadership roles without enough preparation and support by their organizations. In many cases, women leaders experience derailment for multiple factors. For example, one typical combination of factors leading to derailment is when a personal factor, such as a woman's leadership style, has a negative impact on others' perceptions of her, such as her boss. The net effect of the unique challenges that women face in their attempts to advance in the workplace is increased stress and pressure. It is crucial that women develop the capacity to anticipate and successfully navigate these barriers to their career success.

RESILIENCY AS AN ANTIDOTE

The perspective of Oprah in reframing adversity to an opportunity is the essence of resiliency. In the past 40 years, the positive psychology movement has made a significant contribution to the human condition by better defining the factors and variables that enable people to successfully navigate significant challenges and thrive. Resilient people learn from their challenges, make choices about their future, and take deliberate action to move forward. Rather than merely waiting for tough times to happen, resilient people anticipate adversity and prepare for it. When faced with adversity, these individuals experience a less dramatic downturn in their functioning and are less likely to get trapped in the negative emotions they experience.

While some people seem to be naturally resilient, it is a capability that can be developed by anyone who makes a commitment to practice specific strategies. Developing resiliency resources and skills in advance of a career setback can serve as a powerful antidote to future challenges and contribute to women's success. In a 2012 study that involved interviews with 250 senior female leaders, McKinsey & Company discovered that the three most important qualities that contributed to women's success are resilience, grit, and confidence. These qualities are also important for women who are entrepreneurs. Researcher Rania Habiby-Anderson interviewed 250 successful female career women and entrepreneurs in Africa, Asia, Latin America, Eastern Europe, and the Middle East, discovering that resilience and tenacity are critical for overcoming obstacles and achieving success.

DECLINE, SURVIVE, OR THRIVE: THREE VIGNETTES

Consider the cases of three women who faced derailment: Maria, Barbara, and Yolanda. All three were highly qualified, with a solid history of achievement. Maria faced some significant challenges in her role as an external consultant while Barbara and Yolanda struggled to navigate their challenges in full-time internal positions. All three women faced career challenges for differing reasons. They were either asked to resign or potentially face termination as an outcome. However, the outcomes of their stories are significantly different based on their mindset and how they navigated these challenging situations. One woman's career declines, another survives, and the third thrives after a career setback.

DECLINE: THE CASE OF MARIA

Maria was a self-employed human resource (HR) consultant engaged by a fairly new professional services start-up to establish the HR recruiting function. The company had grown quickly in its first two years but had reached the point where a lack of formal internal structures, policies, and infrastructure support was limiting its growth. Up to this point, HR functions such as recruiting and compensation had been left to the discretion of each manager. Maria's client contact, the HR director, was excited to hire Maria because of her broad experience and upbeat personality, which would be a good fit for the organizational culture. The HR director asked Maria to help design critical processes and forms, and drive the implementation. Winning this project represented a significant success for Maria in her new consulting business, as most of the initial client projects she had completed in the past year since starting her business were small in scope and billable revenue.

For the first six months, Maria hit the ground running as she sought to address some of the most critical needs of the organization. She interviewed all of the senior leadership team, including the CEO, to determine the most critical issues to address in a structured recruiting process. With these insights, she focused on creating policies and managerial training programs to bring more consistency to recruiting. Because everything was being built from the ground up, Maria worked long hours each day as well as on weekends. But despite her exhaustion, she was still experiencing the excitement of a new client project and earning significant revenue.

Despite an initially positive reaction when she announced the new recruitment processes, few managers adhered to the new policies Maria proposed. Among the resisters were several senior leaders who actively ignored these new policies and allowed their direct reports to ignore them. In design meetings, she noticed strange nonverbal reactions to her proposed changes when she mentioned her client contact by name, but quickly ignored them. Given her relative lack of experience as an external consultant, Maria had little experience managing such a sensitive situation. She began to become more frustrated and overly assertive in meetings with managers during the rollout phase. Her frustration created a pattern in which stakeholder resistance caused her to become more demanding in requesting compliance with the new policies.

Her inability to achieve success with this critical project and an authoritative communication style led to a significant disagreement with her client contact. On numerous occasions, Maria raised the issue with her client contact about the lack of support for the projects she was responsible for. In one particular meeting, she became emotional and defensive when she had to explain why she had not finished the implementation of the recruiting system. That meeting did not go well. For the next several days, Maria frequently worried about the project, her role, and mistakes she could have inadvertently made. She began to feel very anxious about the possibility of losing this opportunity. Maria had let go of smaller projects with other clients to be able to focus entirely on this client because of its large scope. Her feelings of anxiety led her to distance herself from family and friends, and she began waking up early with fears about being fired.

Unfortunately, her greatest fear came true one Friday afternoon when her client explained that her consulting services were no longer needed. She was told that she made missteps in her frustrated attempts to enlist support from two senior executives who had not bought into the vision for a new recruiting process. Her client also explained that Maria reacted defensively to feedback.

Maria struggled after losing the project. She continued to feel angry with her client, since she felt deceived about being reassured that the changes she was implementing were on track. In retrospect, she wondered whether the reputation of her client contact might have contributed to the lack of support from the organization's stakeholders for the changes she proposed. Maria isolated herself from friends and professional colleagues in the weeks that followed. Several weeks passed with no client projects or revenue despite her efforts to reach out to potential client leads. During this period, she questioned whether she was cut out for self-employment and the challenges of navigating client political dynamics. Her diminished confidence in her own skills limited her willingness to approach prospective new customers.

Since she was not gaining any new consulting projects, Maria began exploring job announcements and halfheartedly sending out résumés. She alternated between feeling sadness and anger about losing this project after a successful launch of her consulting practice and fear for the future in light of a tight economy. Maria's health suffered as she gained weight and looked exhausted. After several months of sending out résumés and responding to online job postings, Maria finally received an offer for a human resources generalist role in a small company. Reluctantly, she accepted this role with an overwhelming sense of confusion about how she ended up in this position after being on such a fast track in her career.

Maria's inexperience with challenging client political dynamics and lack of skills in sustaining her resiliency contributed to a downward spiral in her career viability.

SURVIVE: THE CASE OF BARBARA

The Chief Executive Officer (CEO) of a financial services firm hired Barbara as Chief Financial Officer (CFO) to bring more financial rigor and structure to the organization. While the company had grown despite loose or nonexistent financial policies and practices, the CEO realized that they needed to institute new practices to support a more intentional growth agenda. The former CFO had focused on the treasury function and largely ignored budgeting and finance. The CEO hired her to clean up a loose and haphazard culture among a senior leadership team known for a relaxed attitude toward financial performance and accountability.

While the senior management team was friendly toward her in the first month, her initial attempts to institute structured budgeting starting with top executives were met with indifference and covert resistance. In several meetings, Barbara's direct style in openly challenging her peers was not well received. As a result, the management team made decisions without her involvement that had significant financial implications. She grew increasingly frustrated and raised the issue with the CEO. The CEO's aversion to conflict proved to be a significant barrier to raising and addressing tough issues among the senior management team.

After three months on the job, Barbara began to question why she had taken this job and struggled with how to move forward. Around this time, the CEO indirectly mentioned that things were not working out as planned, and unless she could build more alignment with her colleagues on the senior management team, she would be asked to leave. This news was tough for Barbara, triggering more stress and anxiety for several weeks. In some instances, she would wake very early in the morning and rehash the conversation in her mind. She felt embarrassed, causing her to isolate herself from her friends and pretend that everything was okay. Barbara began a downward spiral of negative self-talk, more embarrassment, and increasing isolation.

Eventually, Barbara heeded the CEO's advice and made an effort to improve her relationship with her peers, which had limited success. She started reaching out to her peers on the executive team to understand their priorities and make an attempt to build relationships. After several attempts, she began to gain traction with two of the seven executives regarding their portfolios, building trust, and enlisting their support for her financial accountability initiative. As a result, Barbara felt less isolated and marginalized during the senior management team meetings. But she gave up on the others and decided to focus on moving her efforts forward with the limited support she was able to establish. Barbara maintained a sense of frustration with her organization, particularly her manager, and was asked to resign several months later. She was unable to overcome the CEO's negative perception despite her progress in establishing workable relationships with two colleagues. Fortunately, several colleagues from a former job were able to help her find a new CFO position in an organization within the same industry. Despite landing in a new role that seemed to be a better fit, Barbara had become more passive and less willing to take risks. She was still unsure how her former job had derailed and what she might do differently to prevent it in the future.

Barbara's situation was one where she demonstrated a foundational level of resiliency, and thus survived the career challenges. While she survived, Barbara still felt impaired by the experience.

THRIVE: THE CASE OF YOLANDA

Yolanda faced a different set of challenges. She was a young lobbyist hired by a utility company to establish a presence in Washington, DC. Congress was considering an increasing number of regulatory bills, causing her organization's leaders to recognize a need to have a voice in the process. Because she had experience interacting with politicians in past jobs, the process of influencing the legislative agenda was among her major strengths. Yolanda's manager, the general counsel, was based in the Midwest along with all of the other senior leaders in the firm.

Yolanda's first challenge was trying to establish a relationship with her manager despite not being in the same office. Another challenge was trying to create a government affairs office in a company that had no experience with such a function. Her challenges were made more complex by not having ready access to some key leadership stakeholders, all of whom were based in the corporate office. Perhaps her most substantial challenge was based on her youthful appearance and lack of assertiveness in engaging some of the corporate executives to formulate consistent policy positions.

After some early wins establishing internal processes for the newly created government relations function, she hit some snags. Yolanda had scheduled a meeting with several executives to get their input and reach consensus on an approach to an emerging effort to increase regulation of their industry. The meeting started off positively, but quickly derailed as several executives and the CEO refused to compromise. Yolanda's attempts to facilitate the conversation failed as the executives ignored her and continued to debate the policy issues. Once the meeting ended, she felt overwhelmed and embarrassed that she had allowed it to derail, unsure of how she could have changed the outcome. Because a bill was being introduced later that week in Congress, reaching internal consensus on a policy position was critical to be able to influence legislators' stance on a crucial new regulation. However, despite her efforts to engage key stakeholders in the days after the meeting, she was unable to formulate a consensus among leaders about her organization's position. Unfortunately, the worst-case scenario occurred when the bill came up to vote in a committee and passed, ultimately resulting in costly new regulations impacting her organization.

Feeling like a failure, Yolanda reached out to her manager for support. Her manager had little awareness of the legislative process but was able to share with Yolanda how frustrated the senior leadership team was with her that they had missed the opportunity to influence the nature of the regulations being proposed. The conversation with her focused on how Yolanda needed to push back on the senior leaders and challenge them to move beyond their deeply held positions. She felt frustrated and misunderstood, explaining that she did not have a management title and legitimacy to be able to challenge the Chief Executive Officer (CEO) and the leadership team. Yolanda worried that despite her best efforts, the lack of support from her manager and lack of organizational awareness of her function would lead to her losing her job.

After a few days of feeling like she was on an emotional roller coaster, she reached out to several colleagues in lobbying roles to get perspective on the situation. Reaching out for support was the very action she needed to take to feel validated. One friend, in particular, had experienced a very similar challenge in her last role. Yolanda was immensely grateful that this friend shared so openly about her struggle and the lessons she learned. One of her friends suggested she might want to hire a coach to build her confidence to assert her ideas with senior leaders as well as educate her company about the government relations role. Yolanda liked the idea of having a trusted supporter to help her have a greater impact.

Yolanda took a chance and asked her manager to pay for her to work with a coach. She was determined to learn from this painful experience and emerge stronger than ever in her career. The coach began the engagement by administering some personality assessments, as well as conducting a 360-degree assessment to collect perceptions of key professional stakeholders about her behavior. Reading the feedback report was painful, but her coach helped her work through her feelings of inadequacy and anger to identify some valuable insights. Yolanda realized how she became passive when she felt overwhelmed and expected others to solve her problems. She began to realize some of the cultural norms associated with how her organization viewed women and strategies she could use to gain support from critical male stakeholders. The coach helped Yolanda experiment with new ways of communicating and deepening the relationship with her manager as well as several executives who could act as champions for her efforts. Also, the coach helped Yolanda formulate a longer-term vision for her career and clarify her needs for support and work and life integration.

After several months, Yolanda had made substantial improvements in her impact. She and her manager were more in agreement about what constituted success in her role and the support she needed in engaging senior leaders. Yolanda also built strong relationships with a couple of well-regarded executives. She felt more assertive and confident in fulfilling her role while recognizing when she needed to tap the formal power held by her internal advocates to push back on several executives' resistance to change. Yolanda's decision to work with a coach paid off. She was more productive and happier in her current role, and she had a clearer sense of where she was going in her career.

Yolanda faced some significant challenges introducing change in her organization, but was able to overcome these challenges resiliently and thrive.

DECLINE, SURVIVE, OR THRIVE: THE RESILIENCY FRAMEWORK

The women in these case studies represent three contrasting outcomes in coping with career challenges. Maria's fixed mindset and inability to resiliently deal with her challenges led to a downward spiral in her career and other domains of her life, causing her to succumb to career derailment. Barbara demonstrated a level of resiliency that helped her survive the experience and return to a level of functioning consistent with life before the setback. However, Yolanda's story embodied the essence of resiliency, powerfully embracing a growth mindset and demonstrating what it means to thrive in the face of near derailment.

The Resiliency Framework is a set of six strategies that will help when navigating a current career challenge, or help to build resiliency to avoid or minimize career challenges in the future. Challenges include both small issues, such as dealing with computer challenges, and larger issues, such as conflict with a peer.

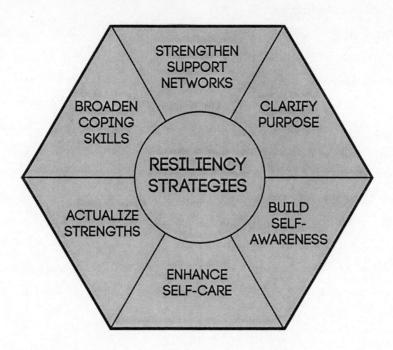

The strategies in the framework include:

- **Strengthen Support Networks**—Proactively increase the breadth and depth of your support networks to help you maintain or regain balance in the midst of adversity.

- **Clarify Purpose**—Focus on understanding your values, passions, vision, mission, and goals to boost your sense of optimism, align your behavior, and take action.

- **Build Self-Awareness**—Develop an awareness of your thoughts, emotions, and development needs to improve your capacity to consciously manage your behavior.

- **Enhance Self-Care**—Improve your physical, emotional, and spiritual well-being to increase your energy and inoculate yourself against stress.

- **Actualize Strengths**—Maximize your strengths to build confidence, gain the courage to take risks, and achieve greater results.

- **Broaden Coping Skills**—Strengthen the skills necessary to reframe the challenge and make intentional choices that lead to growth and thriving, not just surviving.

This framework presents a dynamic range of options for gaining insight and taking action. To fully thrive in a career, it is important to possess a baseline level of functioning in each of the six strategies. Someone may perform well in some strategies and only need to focus on the weak areas.

The following table summarizes the presence of these Resiliency Strategies in each of the three cases.

	THRIVE YOLANDA	SURVIVE BARBARA	DECLINE MARTA
STRENGTHEN SUPPORT NETWORKS	Engaged support from broad sources; two-way exchange of support	Periodically engaged her limited support network	Isolated herself
CLARIFY PURPOSE	Clear about her career vision and values; consciously chose career options	Clarified the next steps in her career and how it fit with her core values	Unsure of her vision; focused only on the needs of potential employers

	THRIVE YOLANDA	SURVIVE BARBARA	DECLINE MARIA
BUILD SELF-AWARENESS	Consistently reflected on her thoughts, feelings, and strengths; asked for feedback from others	Periodically assessed her strengths and abilities; receptive to feedback if offered	Lacked awareness of herself; overly focused on her weaknesses; threatened by feedback
ENHANCE SELF-CARE	Intentionally focused on physical, emotional, and spiritual wellness; managed stress well	Occasionally practiced physical care, including diet and exercise, but not consistent	Neglected her needs for adequate sleep, diet, and exercise; constantly tired and stressed
ACTUALIZE STRENGTHS	Developed greater awareness of her strengths and opportunities to use them	Aware of strengths but settled for situations that did not optimize them	Lacked awareness of strengths; settled for career situations that didn't fit her
BROADEN COPING SKILLS	Quickly reframed negative situation; strong growth mindset	Slowly reframed situations and took action; growth-oriented	Mired in sadness and resentment; stuck in a fixed mindset

One of the biggest factors that determined the outcome for these three women was their mindset. When women facing career setbacks embrace a growth mindset, they are better equipped to anticipate, navigate, and be transformed by the challenges. Whether women are working with a coach or on their own, a growth mindset enables them to anticipate and prepare for potential challenges, as well as reduce the impact and duration of adverse experiences.

THE ROAD AHEAD: HOW TO USE THIS BOOK

This book was designed to be a practical guidebook combined with inspiring stories to motivate action. Together, the stories and strategies provide a pathway to greater resiliency.

Chapter 2 provides the foundation with a self-assessment and the creation of a plan for moving forward. The self-assessment provides the information needed to make decisions on which of the six Resiliency Strategies need attention. The Resiliency Action Plan functions as an overall guide to track the completion of the principal actions associated with the selected Resiliency Strategies. The Resiliency Action Plan combined with an introduction to techniques for self-coaching will provide the focus to navigate the rest of the book.

Chapters 3 through 14 consist of six Resiliency Strategy chapters and six narrative chapters focused on stories written by women who resiliently navigated challenges in their careers. Each chapter associated with the Resiliency Strategies includes:

- A case example of a woman who faced career adversity.

- Derailment triggers consisting of work challenges that could lead to derailment if not successfully addressed.

- Derailment trigger questions to explore in order to avoid career setbacks.

- An in-depth explanation of the Resiliency Strategy and the five action steps to take.

- An example of how the woman applied the Resiliency Strategy.

- Detailed instructions on how to complete the five actions associated with each Resiliency Strategy.

- A Resiliency Action Plan Summary Worksheet at the end of the chapter that allows you to set goals to take action and make progress.

- A list of online resources and software applications that can be accessed from electronic devices to explore each strategy more fully.

Six women from around the world wrote the narrative chapters based on their experiences navigating career challenges. These women represent a wide range of ages, professions, and geographic locations. These powerful stories can be used to learn how these women applied the Resiliency Strategies and the wisdom they gained in their journeys.

Chapter 15 concludes the book with a call to action for women, people developers, organizational leaders, and men. The final sections of the book are an acknowledgment section and a notes section.

There are two ways to use this book. The Resiliency Strategies will help women build internal and external resources to navigate challenges and prevent career setbacks. Alternatively, for a woman experiencing career challenges, this book will provide specific strategies to rebound and thrive. Women will want to start by completing the resiliency self-assessment in chapter 2 and then deciding which strategies they should include in the Resiliency Action Plan. The women's narrative stories augment the Resiliency Strategy chapters by enhancing motivation to navigate challenges.

People developers who coach and mentor women, including human resource, talent management, career development, and coaching professionals, will gain useful insights into the experiences of women facing setbacks and Resiliency Strategies to help women thrive. For coaches, this book contains insights from research on coaching competencies that are particularly critical for women facing derailment. The Resiliency Strategy chapters offer practical ideas for helping clients enhance their resiliency.

Organizational leaders will benefit from this book and be able to implement suggestions that will help any organization fully utilize the talent that women bring to the workforce. Chapters 2 through 14 provide insights into the challenges that women face in the workplace. Chapter 15 provides suggestions for how to help women overcome those challenges. This book will help organizational leaders better integrate women into the workforce by creating an environment that supports working women. The book will assist academic institutions in creating curricula that will better equip women to understand the challenges they will face in the workforce and how to build resiliency. The book will assist in creating curricula for future leaders and coaches to help them support and develop women leaders.

This book will benefit men in two ways. It can help men enhance their career resiliency, and give them a glimpse into the personalities and experiences that women face in the workplace. The Resiliency Strategies also apply to men as they contain good practical insights for anyone. Men play a critical role in supporting their female colleagues' success in the workplace, and this book offers valuable insights on what women face.

Ultimately, viewing adversity as a growth opportunity determines how you will cope with career challenges. Oprah Winfrey embraced this perspective and thrived to create both a multimillion-dollar brand and an enduring legacy for helping women. A growth mindset, along with the Resiliency Framework and supporting strategies, will launch and sustain the journey toward career success.

TWO

LAYING THE FOUNDATION: RESILIENCY ACTION PLAN

You must do the thing you think you cannot do.
— Eleanor Roosevelt

Conventional wisdom has long argued that writing down one's goals is essential to achieving them. A recent study has provided empirical support for this practice. Dr. Gail Matthews conducted a study in 2014 that demonstrated the impact of writing down goals, identifying specific actions to fulfill these goals, and establishing accountability with others. In her study, she recruited a diverse sample of 267 participants and randomly assigned them to one of five groups:

- Group 1 simply thought about goals they hoped to achieve in a four-week period and evaluated them based on difficulty, importance, and expectations of success.

- Group 2 volunteers wrote their goals and evaluated them similar to group 1.

- Group 3 wrote their goals, evaluated them, and identified actions to achieve them.

- Group 4 used the same approach as group 3, with the added level of sharing their commitments with friends.

- Group 5 used the same approach as group 4, but also sent weekly updates to their friends.

The results of her study were striking. Participants in the first group achieved 43 percent of their goals. Research participants in the fifth group achieved an average of 76 percent of their goals.

This chapter explores four key steps to help you enhance your resiliency consistent with Dr. Matthews' powerful research:

1. Complete a self-assessment that will allow you to identify the Resiliency Strategies you most need to focus on right now.

2. Create the Resiliency Action Plan to guide your exploration of the activities associated with each Resiliency Strategy.

3. Implement the specific Resiliency Strategies you have selected and update the Resiliency Action Plan Summary Worksheet at the end of the chapter.

4. Use self-coaching as a way of helping yourself take action with your Resiliency Action Plan and goals.

STEP 1: ASSESSING YOURSELF

In this step, each of the six Resiliency Strategies is explored in depth. As you read each strategy, assess how well you are currently functioning with each of these strategies based on past behavior. You will have the option to indicate whether you are thriving, surviving, or declining in the way you function with each strategy. Once you complete the assessment, you will be able to determine potentially vulnerable areas and choose specific Resiliency Strategies in step two.

STRATEGY 1: STRENGTHEN SUPPORT NETWORKS

With this strategy, you will increase the breadth and depth of your support networks to help you maintain or regain balance in the midst of adversity. There are five actions associated with this strategy:

- Determine the kind of support you need.

- Assess the quality of your support network.

- Deepen your relationship with people in your network.

- Maintain your professional network on a regular basis.

- Identify ways to broaden your network.

Social support is an integral component of coping successfully with adversity, regaining resiliency, and thriving. It primarily consists of information that people receive about being loved, supported, and belonging to a network of others. Perceived support consists of awareness of your sources of support and is particularly important when people first encounter an adverse situation. One of the first things people do when making sense of the threat is make an instant appraisal of the support available, both internal and external resources. If people think they have enough resources to cope, including social support, it allows them to shift their perspective of the adverse situation from a threat to a challenge. Most people will approach a threat head-on if they perceive they are supported in a way that will result in better outcomes.

The reverse is also true. If a woman views an adverse situation as a threat, she tends to engage in emotional fight-or-flight behavior. People who lack sufficient social support networks often isolate themselves, which contributes to depression and helplessness. Highly resilient people strengthen their support networks before adversity happens so that the safety net is ready should they face tough times.

Consider your social support network and reflect on the following descriptions of each level in the self-assessment.

- Thriving: You have a network with breadth, including people from multiple domains (e.g., work, personal, professional, industry or sector), and depth, consisting of varying levels of emotional connection (e.g., close confidantes, advocates, or acquaintances). You regularly engage with your support networks to maintain the relationship and reciprocate in these relationships to support others' interests. In the midst of career adversity, there are a variety of people you could reach out to for emotional support or help in navigating the challenge.

- Surviving: You have support networks that are more limited in either breadth or depth. You focus primarily on fulfilling your needs in your interactions and infrequently maintain the relationships in your network. In the midst of career adversity, there is one person in your network you could reach out to for emotional support or help in navigating the challenge.

- Declining: You have a narrow or nonexistent support network and rarely stay connected with the support networks you do have unless you face a significant challenge. You may find it difficult to identify anyone you might reach out to for support in the face of adversity.

Refer to the following checklist and identify your current level of functioning for this Resiliency Strategy.

THRIVING	SURVIVING	DECLINING

STRATEGY 2: CLARIFY PURPOSE

With this strategy you will focus on understanding your values, passions, vision, mission, and goals to boost your sense of optimism, align your behavior, and take action. There are five actions associated with this strategy:

- Identify the core values that make you unique.

- Understand the passions and interests that motivate you.

- Develop a clear sense of vision for your life and career.

- Create a mission aligned with your values, passions, and vision.

- Implement goals that enable you to accomplish your mission.

This strategy is effective because it draws upon a number of internal traits and factors contributing to resiliency. Establishing a vision for your career and life helps you to develop and sustain optimism, a key determinant of your willingness to take action toward your goals. Optimism is a belief in a positive future. People give up and get depressed, particularly when faced with tough times, when they lack optimism. The opposite of optimism is a feeling of helplessness and pessimism. Numerous studies have linked optimism to a number of positive outcomes, including health. Psychologist Martin Seligman suggests that optimists enjoy a number of health-related benefits, including fewer diseases and stronger immune systems. A clear vision and connection to your passions triggers positive emotions and helps you keep perspective when faced with tough times in your work. As noted psychologist Barbara Fredrickson suggests, resilient people use positive emotions to sustain themselves. Clarifying your purpose is a form of problem-oriented coping that has been shown to enhance your resiliency.

Consider your mission, vision, values, and passions, and reflect on the following descriptions of each level in the self-assessment.

- Thriving: You have identified your values and passions, created your vision (long-term) and mission (short-term), and have set goals to achieve your life and career aspirations. Your values, passions, vision, mission and goals are aligned with your current role.

- Surviving: You have short-term clarity about your values, passions, and career, and may be in a role that is aligned. You are unclear about a longer-term vision that aligns with your values and passions. You are without a vision, mission, or goals that will move you toward your longer-term life and career aspirations.

- Declining: You are not clear on your values and passions. In the short term, you are unsure if your current role is aligned with your values and passions. You have not identified your vision, mission, and goals that will move you toward your longer-term life and career aspirations.

Refer to the following checklist and identify your current level of functioning for this Resiliency Strategy.

THRIVING	SURVIVING	DECLINING

STRATEGY 3: BUILD SELF-AWARENESS
With this strategy, you will develop an awareness of your thoughts, emotions, and development needs to improve your capacity to manage your behavior consciously. There are five actions associated with this strategy:

- Solicit feedback from others about your strengths and development areas and create development goals.

- Realize how your thoughts influence your emotions and behaviors.

- Understand your emotional hot buttons.

- Make conscious choices about your reactions to others.

- Monitor your level of resiliency and take actions to increase resiliency.

Consider the metaphor of a thermostat. This device helps maintain a constant environment in a room by detecting changes in temperature. If it becomes too cool or warm, the thermostat kicks on to make adjustments. In similar ways, when you increase your self-awareness, you are better able to maintain your resiliency by noticing your inner emotions and outer behavior.

The list below summarizes three levels of effectiveness as it relates to self-awareness. Consider your self-awareness practices and reflect on the following descriptions of each level in the self-assessment:

- Thriving: You proactively solicit feedback from others and are aware of your strengths and development areas. You have created development goals and are focused on improving your development areas. You are self-aware and know how your emotions influence your behaviors. You make conscious choices about your reactions to others.

- Surviving: You have some awareness of your development areas based on feedback from others. You may have development goals that you focus on inconsistently. While you can be self-aware, at times you are inadvertently triggered emotionally and respond reactively.

- Declining: You have limited awareness of your development areas. You may not have development goals and rarely engage in development activities. You can easily be triggered emotionally and react negatively.

Refer to the following checklist and identify your current level of functioning for this Resiliency Strategy.

THRIVING	SURVIVING	DECLINING

STRATEGY 4: ENHANCE SELF-CARE

With this strategy, you will focus on your physical, emotional, and spiritual well-being to increase your energy and inoculate yourself against stress. There are five actions associated with this strategy:

- Assess your physical, emotional, and spiritual well-being.

- Implement actions to improve your physical health.

- Integrate activities that restore your emotional strength.

- Incorporate spiritual practices into your schedule.

- Effectively integrate the time spent on work and self-care activities.

Physical, emotional, and spiritual well-being are linked to developing and maintaining your resiliency. According to physician Dr. David Hellerstein, "Physical toughening and tempering are key components of resilience ... people who are physically toughened can withstand prolonged stress better than those who aren't. Not only does physical fitness make for stronger hearts, lower blood pressure, and lower blood sugar, as well as directly decreasing anxiety and depression and improving sleep—but exercise also increases the levels of neurotrophic factors ... which improve brain health."

Spirituality is an important way that people draw meaning from their lives and maintain their perspective on what is most important. Therefore, developing a fulfilling spiritual life can play an important role in building your capacity to powerfully adapt to tough times.

Because soldiers in the military face unique hardships that can result in debilitating post-traumatic stress and suicide, significant investments have been made in branches of the U.S. military to build resiliency. The U.S. Air Force offers training programs that include a component on spiritual resilience as a means for supporting the development of resiliency for its soldiers. Emotional well-being is based on your awareness of and ability to manage the range of emotions you may face when encountering tough times. Since your thoughts trigger emotions, the way you talk to yourself when you face challenges can play a critical role in sustaining your emotional well-being.

The list below summarizes three levels of effectiveness as it relates to self-care. Consider your efforts to maintain your physical resiliency and reflect on the following descriptions of each level in the self-assessment:

- Thriving: You regularly assess your physical, emotional, and spiritual well-being. You consistently implement physical, emotional, and spiritual self-care activities. You are able to effectively integrate the time you spend on work and self-care activities to increase your energy and reduce stress.

- Surviving: You infrequently assess your physical, emotional, and spiritual well-being. You may implement one or two self-care activities, whether physical, emotional, or spiritual, but you do not focus on all three. You are not always able to effectively integrate the time you spend on work and self-care activities, causing your energy and stress levels to be inconsistent.

- Declining: You rarely assess your physical, emotional, and spiritual well-being. You infrequently implement any physical, emotional, or spiritual activities. You are not able to effectively integrate the time you spend on work and self-care activities, causing your energy level to be low and your stress level to be high.

Refer to the following checklist and identify your current level of functioning for this Resiliency Strategy.

THRIVING	SURVIVING	DECLINING

STRATEGY 5: ACTUALIZE STRENGTHS

With this strategy, you will maximize your strengths to build confidence, gain the courage to take risks, and achieve greater results. There are five actions associated with this strategy:

- Identify your unique strengths.

- Determine ways to use your strengths more fully on a regular basis.

- Identify others who can augment your weaknesses.

- Find ways to develop your strengths.

- Identify other key factors that help you feel confident and powerful.

This strategy draws upon research into self-efficacy, also known as self-confidence, and growth mindsets. Self-efficacy is a person's belief in their capabilities. When people have the right level of self-efficacy, they can initiate actions and sustain their effort in the face of difficulties. Further, they feel more empowered to take control of events in their lives. Self-efficacy also influences the choices people make, the goals they set, the amount of effort they invest in a task, how they think about something, and the stress they experience. With a strong sense of self-efficacy, you will feel confident about your abilities and envision success when faced with tough times, which better equips you to assert your ideas and opinions with others. Your belief in yourself, combined with a growth mindset, will form a positive, self-fulfilling prophecy.

The list below summarizes three levels of effectiveness as it relates to actualizing your strengths. Consider your beliefs associated with your strengths and abilities, and reflect on the following descriptions of each level in the self-assessment.

- Thriving: You have a clear awareness of your strengths and other factors that enable you to feel confident and assertive when taking risks. You regularly invest in developing your strengths and leveraging the talents of others to augment your weaknesses. You are consistently confident and courageous in taking risks to achieve results in your role.

- Surviving: You understand your strengths and find ways to use them, but may not be consistent in your efforts to develop them. There may be instances where you engage the talents of others, but not consistently. In some instances you are unwilling to assert yourself and your ideas.

- Declining: You are unaware of your strengths and therefore do not invest time in developing them or leveraging the talents of others to augment your weaknesses. You often find yourself in situations that do not play to your strengths and lack confidence in asserting yourself or your ideas.

Refer to the following checklist and identify your current level of functioning for this Resiliency Strategy.

THRIVING	SURVIVING	DECLINING

STRATEGY 6: BROADEN COPING SKILLS

With this strategy, you will proactively strengthen the skills necessary to reframe your challenge and make intentional choices that lead to growth and thriving, not just surviving. There are five actions associated with this strategy:

- Embrace a growth mindset in the way you talk to yourself about your challenges.

- Use scenario planning to envision the best and worst cases.

- Identify effective ways to get perspective on your challenges.

- Identify aspects of challenges that you can and cannot control.

- Increase the frequency of positive emotions and decrease the frequency of negative emotions.

Coping skills, particularly problem-centered skills, are essential to thrive since they determine the way you perceive a tough situation, as well as the actions you take to either prevent or recover from tough times. Examples of problem-centered coping skills include scenario planning or identifying aspects of a challenge you have control over. Even emotion-based coping strategies, such as expressing your negative emotions or actively increasing the frequency of positive emotions, can play a role in coping with a challenge when the situation first occurs. People who are less resilient tend to get trapped in their emotions, leading to passivity, ignoring the reality of the situation, and sinking into victimization. In addition, the way you cope is linked to your confidence in yourself and your ability to handle tough circumstances.

The list below summarizes three levels of effectiveness as it relates to coping strategies. Consider your coping approach in the face of adversity and reflect on the following descriptions of each level in the self-assessment.

- Thriving: You are skilled at consistently viewing challenging situations as growth opportunities and evoking positive emotions in yourself to enable you to resiliently navigate your initial emotional reactions to tough times. You practice problem-centered coping approaches such as scenario planning, gaining perspective, and identifying situational factors you can and cannot control. Most of the time you make intentional choices about your future.

- Surviving: You may initially get mired in your emotions when facing a tough situation, but eventually use problem-focused coping strategies such as scenario planning, gaining perspective, and identifying situational factors you can and cannot control. In using these coping strategies, you sometimes make intentional choices about your future.

- Declining: You often get trapped in your emotions, and resist opportunities to grow. You may feel as though you have no options regarding your future and may feel stuck and resentful.

Refer to the following checklist and identify your current level of functioning for this Resiliency Strategy.

THRIVING	SURVIVING	DECLINING

STEP 2: CREATING YOUR RESILIENCY ACTION PLAN

Now that you have reviewed each of the six strategies and identified your current level of functioning, you are ready to complete the Resiliency Action Plan. (**Table 2.1**) This plan will provide guidance and personal accountability for completing your targeted Resiliency Strategies. In order to determine the specific Resiliency Strategies you want to focus on and the appropriate sequence, you may want to consider the following guidelines:

- If you assessed all of the Resiliency Strategies as thriving, consider whether any specific strategies could be proactively strengthened in light of a unique challenge you are facing. For example, if you are

Table 2.1

Resiliency Action Plan		
Activities	**Target Date**	**Complete?**
Strengthen support networks	Rating:	
_ Determine the kind of support you need		
_ Assess the quality of your support network		
_ Deepen your relationship with your network		
_ Maintain your professional network		
_ Identify ways to broaden your network		
Clarify purpose	Rating:	
_ Identify the core values that make you unique		
_ Understand your passions and interests		
_ Develop a clear sense of vision for your life/career		
_ Create a mission aligned with values/passions		
_ Implement goals that enable your mission		
Build self-awareness	Rating:	
_ Solicit feedback from others/create goals		
_ Realize how thoughts influence emotions		
_ Understand your emotional hot buttons		
_ Make conscious choices about your reactions		
_ Monitor your level of resiliency		
Enhance self-care	Rating:	
_ Assess physical/emotional/spiritual well-being		
_ Implement actions to improve your physical health		
_ Integrate activities that restore emotional health		
_ Incorporate spiritual practices into your schedule		
_ Effectively integrate time spent on work/self-care		
Actualize strengths	Rating:	
_ Identify your unique strengths		
_ Determine ways to use your strengths more fully		
_ Identify others who can augment your weaknesses		
_ Find ways to develop your strengths		
_ Identify factors that help you feel confident		
Broaden coping skills	Rating:	
_ Embrace a growth mindset in your self-talk		
_ Use scenario planning to envision the best/worst		
_ Identify effective ways to get perspective on challenges		
_ Identify aspects of challenges you can/cannot control		
_ Increase the freq. of positive emotions		

facing a promotion, it may be useful to revisit enhancing self-care to ensure that you are physically ready to cope with the additional stress you may face in that role. Also, it may be helpful to review the derailment triggers in each chapter to help you anticipate challenges that could develop.

- If you assessed any of the Resiliency Strategies as declining or surviving, focus first on those that are declining. By addressing your weakest areas and taking the recommended actions, you may actually improve your functioning with the other strategies. For example, when you enhance self-care you may concurrently broaden your coping skills. After you complete the Resiliency Strategies and actions associated with your weakest areas, take the self-assessment again to determine if there have been any improvements for other strategies you initially rated as surviving.

This worksheet contains the following elements:

- **Rating** represents your evaluation completed in the last section of the level at which you are functioning for the respective Resiliency Strategy (e.g., thriving, surviving, or declining).

- **Activities** represent the specific activities associated with the Resiliency Strategy that you are planning on completing to enhance your functioning for this strategy. Place a check mark next to each activity you will complete. If you are unclear about a particular action and its purpose, you may want to first read the chapter and activity description.

- **Target date** for completion represents your best estimate for when you want to have completed the activity described in each of the following chapters associated with each of the actions. In choosing a target date, be sure to allow yourself enough time to complete the activity as well as reflect upon insights you have gained.

- **Complete** indicates whether you have completed the activity identified. Check this when you have completed the activity.

Table 2.2

Resiliency Action Plan for Maria		
Activities	Target Date	Complete?
Strengthen support networks	Rating: Declining	
✓ Determine the kind of support you need	11/30	
✓ Assess the quality of your support network	11/30	
✓ Deepen your relationship with your network	11/30	
✓ Maintain your professional network	11/30	
✓ Identify ways to broaden your network	11/30	
Clarify purpose	Rating: Surviving	
_ Identify the core values that make you unique		
_ Understand your passions and interests		
_ Develop a clear sense of vision for your life/career		
_ Create a mission aligned with values/passions		
_ Implement goals that enable your mission		
Build self-awareness	Rating: Declining	
✓ Solicit feedback from others/create goals	1/31	
✓ Realize how thoughts influence emotions	1/31	
✓ Understand your emotional hot buttons	1/31	
✓ Make conscious choices about your reactions	1/31	
✓ Monitor your level of resiliency	1/31	
Enhance self-care	Rating: Surviving	
_ Assess physical/emotional/spiritual well-being		
_ Implement actions to improve your physical health		
_ Integrate activities that restore emotional health		
_ Incorporate spiritual practices into your schedule		
_ Effectively integrate time spent on work/self-care		
Actualize strengths	Rating: Declining	
✓ Identify your unique strengths	3/15	
✓ Determine ways to use your strengths more fully	3/15	
✓ Identify others who can augment your weaknesses	3/15	
✓ Find ways to develop your strengths	3/15	
✓ Identify factors that help you feel confident	3/15	
Broaden coping skills	Rating: Declining	
✓ Embrace a growth mindset in your self-talk	4/30	
✓ Use scenario planning to envision the best/worst	4/30	
✓ Identify effective ways to get perspective on challenges	4/30	
✓ Identify aspects of challenges you can/cannot control	4/30	
✓ Increase the freq. of positive emotions	4/30	

One of the vignettes presented in chapter 1 was the story of Maria, an HR consultant who was struggling in her career. In reflecting on her career and her challenges, Maria completed the assessment in this chapter and realized that four of the six strategies were declining: Strengthen Support Networks, Build Self-Awareness, Actualize Strengths, and Broaden Coping Skills.

Once she created her Resiliency Action Plan (**Table 2.2**), Maria updated it periodically to track her progress and maintain accountability with herself. She set the milestone dates in a way that would drive action and forward movement but not overwhelm her, given other priorities in her life and work. She decided that once she addressed her four most vulnerable strategies, she would again take the self-assessment to determine where she was functioning with the other two Resiliency Strategies.

STEP 3: EXPLORING THE RESILIENCY STRATEGIES

You are now ready to move into action with each of the Resiliency Strategies you identified in step two as being critical. Once you read each of the chapters associated with the Resiliency Strategies you selected, you will gain a clearer sense of the strategy, how it is implemented, and how it may benefit you. Each strategy consists of five activities you can perform to enhance your resiliency. At the conclusion of each activity, you will be invited to capture a SMART goal on the Resiliency Action Plan Summary Worksheet at the end of each strategy chapter. "SMART" refers to a specific format for writing goals in a way that you are more likely to achieve them: S – specific, M – measurable, A – achievable, R – result-focused, and T – time-based. While you will have one Resiliency Action Plan, you will create a Resiliency Action Plan Summary Worksheet for each strategy you explore.

Maria identified four Resiliency Strategies to focus on. The Resiliency Action Plan Summary Worksheet she created after reading chapter 4 (Strengthen Support Networks) is included on the next page (**Table 2.3**).

The Resiliency Action Plan Summary Worksheet (**Table 2.3**) is a

Table 2.3

☑	Maria's Resiliency Action Plan Summary Worksheet	
Activity	**Key Outcome or SMART Goals**	
1	Identify and choose an image consultant and marketing expert by December 15.	
2	Schedule lunch meetings with three former HR colleagues I have lost contact with by December 15.	
3	Schedule one lunch meeting with Susan by December 31 and discover ways I can support her success.	
4	On the first day of each month, starting in January, schedule a lunch meeting with one of my most important clients starting with Tiffany Roberts.	
5	Attend one meeting of the American Society for Healthcare Human Resources Administration in February and meet three new contacts.	

useful way to translate the activities into focused action that will enhance your resiliency. The combination of a clear Resiliency Action Plan, SMART goals that set clear intentions, and self-coaching will make a significant contribution to addressing the vulnerable areas identified in the self-assessment.

STEP 4: MOVING INTO ACTION WITH SELF-COACHING
In step four you are ready to act upon your Resiliency Action Plan and SMART goals. You may choose to work independently, work with others, or engage others to support you and enhance your accountability as needed. Self-coaching is a useful way to move forward and consists of a number of mindsets and practices that will be introduced in this step.

INTRODUCTION TO SELF-COACHING
While most people think of coaching in terms of working with a professional coach toward their development goals, self-coaching is a use-

ful way to enhance your ability to thrive when faced with career adversity. Self-coaching is a method for helping you to reach your potential where you partner with yourself, much as an actual coach would, to motivate yourself, deepen your learning, and ultimately reach your goals.

Two key assumptions that guide professional coaches can also apply to self-coaching. First, coaches make the assumption that their clients hold far more wisdom than their clients perceive in themselves. To unleash this wisdom, good coaches frequently ask nonjudgmental, open-ended questions to help their clients discover this wisdom. When you practice self-coaching, you are more likely to achieve success when you ask yourself great questions that prompt insight instead of judgmental statements that function only to limit your learning. Second, coaches assume that by holding their clients accountable for taking action, they are more likely to gain clarity and insight. Talking incessantly about a challenge often does not translate to moving forward. For you to enhance your career, it's important to hold yourself accountable to your Resiliency Action Plan and achieve your SMART goals.

SELF-COACHING PRACTICES

To gain the most from this book, it is critical to consider how you will use these materials in terms of:

- What venue will you use to perform self-coaching?

- When will you explore and complete the suggested activities, taking into account what else may be happening in your life?

- What tools or support would help you complete these activities?

The venue for self-coaching refers to how you will use these materials to engage with yourself. Examples include asking yourself questions, visualizing yourself taking a specific action or responding powerfully to your challenges, writing your ideas and reflections in a journal, or engaging others in conversation to explore the ideas more fully. Within each of the six strategy chapters that follow, there are five activities, one for each of the five actions that define each Resiliency Strategy. Each of these activities will give you the opportunity to practice your ability to self-coach.

There are three situations when you can perform self-coaching for yourself, including regularly scheduled sessions, ad hoc in-the-moment situations, or following your attempts to try a new behavior. It is helpful to schedule regular sessions to complete activities identified on your Resiliency Action Plan. For example, perhaps Sunday afternoons become the times you set aside time to read the specific chapter, attempt the activities, and coach yourself on your responses. As you implement the Resiliency Strategies and SMART goals you formulated, there will likely be unlimited ad hoc opportunities to coach yourself.

For example, let's say you are interested in increasing the frequency of positive emotions to help you cope more effectively with adversity. Ad hoc self-coaching in this instance might involve noticing the presence of negative emotions and making a choice to experience a positive emotion. In this case, you assume the role of an observer of your actions, which is a very useful tool for creating personal change and deepening your learning. After you complete an action or SMART goal, self-coaching can help deepen your learning and reinforce progress. For example, if one of your SMART goals focuses on deepening relationships with your colleagues, you might do some self-coaching after the meeting. You could reflect on the success of a conversation, insights gained, and any alternative behavior you might try the next time you attempt a similar conversation.

SELF-COACHING SUPPORT

Finally, a component of self-coaching relates to support you provide for yourself as well as support you request from others. Based on the research conducted by Dr. Gail Matthews introduced at the beginning of this chapter, people who enlist the support of friends in the form of accountability are more likely to achieve their goals. Professional coaches often provide support to their clients in many forms, such as:

- Celebrating successes and victories.

- Emotional support and empathy when facing adversity, loss, or overwhelm.

- Accountability support to reinforce key commitments.

- Role modeling of target behaviors.

- Informational support to get information needed to guide decisions.

Consider which forms of support you can provide for yourself and what support you need from others. One easy way to create accountability for yourself is by scheduling time to complete the Resiliency Action Plan and building in rewards for yourself when you complete a SMART goal or achieve a success in building your resiliency. Similar to the support you could receive from a professional coach, enlisting support from trusted friends or colleagues could take multiple forms:

- Sending your completed Resiliency Action Plan and SMART goals to your accountability partners.

- Providing regular updates to your colleagues.

- Asking colleagues to send you a supportive email or text at periodic intervals.

- Inviting colleagues to provide feedback on your progress.

This chapter lays the foundation for action and insight through four key steps. First, by assessing your current level of functioning with each of the six Resiliency Strategies, you are better prepared to identify the strategies you most need to enhance. Second, the Resiliency Action Plan will guide your efforts to complete specific actions linked to the targeted Resiliency Strategies. Third, capturing your SMART goals on the Resiliency Action Plan Summary Worksheet at the end of each strategy chapter will help deepen your commitment to take action. Fourth, with an understanding of self-coaching you are better equipped to complete each of the activities, act upon your SMART goals, deepen your learning, and strengthen your resiliency muscles.

THREE

ANNA'S STORY: SURRENDERING TO VULNERABILITY

BY ANNA STEFFENEY

Vulnerability is not about fear and grief and disappointment. It is the birthplace of everything we are hungry for.
— BRENÉ BROWN

Imagine you are in a small rowboat with two oars to help you travel on a river. The river has tributaries with twists and turns, and with that comes choices. Which direction shall I go? The only way to turn, or make the boat go faster, is to row. This metaphor represents how I felt as I navigated my twenties, rowing as fast as I could and making decisions about which tributaries I wanted to travel down. Later I discovered there might be another way to travel this river of life—by simply pulling the oars in and surrendering.

This image helps me describe my transition in life. Throughout my twenties, I defined myself as a career woman, putting my personal relationships second to my career. I studied finance and technology in college, and my first job was at a large insurance company, part of a rotational leadership trainee program. My first rotation was programming computers in the COBOL language. The leadership development program put me and my career on the fast track. My focus on my career began to change in my early thirties when I started shifting my priorities to having a more balanced life. During this phase I realized I could let the water in the river guide me. The oars were still in the water paddling, but with more thoughtfulness and less speed.

This change didn't happen overnight. It began when I followed my boyfriend, now my husband, to Germany as he began his new job. That first step in my transition from focusing solely on my career to a more balanced focus on career and family was the beginning of my journey of surrendering control. Trusting that I would identify the right destination allowed me to lift the oars out of the water. My transition, while leveraging my resiliency strategies, led me to what I do today as a wife, mother, and entrepreneur. I am focused on improving the lives of working families.

I had been living and working in Germany for five years when I became pregnant. My husband and I were excited to start a family. Soon after I found out, I told my manager. My manager congratulated me and immediately suggested that we find an apprentice to fill my role while I was out on maternity leave. In Germany, I had the legal option to take one year of paid leave and three years of additional job-protected leave. However, I opted to take only one year of paid leave. Fortunately, I didn't have to choose between my career and my child on a daily basis, nor did I feel like I had to divorce myself from my career identity.

Two years later, I had been promoted and relocated to my company's headquarters in the United States. Soon after arriving, I found out that I was pregnant with my second child. I discovered all the corporate benefits my company provided at a human resource meeting, including discounted childcare, backup care, and only four months of paid maternity leave. I wanted my second child to have the same bonding experience as my first. I raised my hand and asked the human resource representative how I could stay home longer than four months. She responded, "If you are conflicted with the decision to come back to work after four months, we offer mental health services." I laughed and responded, "I am not crazy. I just want a few more months of maternity leave."

Needing information about how I could get more than four months of leave, I asked my coworkers. Unfortunately, my coworkers confirmed that I would not be able to take more than four months of maternity leave unless I quit my job. I was shocked by what I learned, and I had to know more. I discovered that most women didn't feel comfortable going to their manager, or even human resources, to discover what their leave options were. Instead, they cornered female coworkers in the bathroom and asked how the maternity leave process worked. Women were often told to keep the fact that they were pregnant hidden for as long as possible. This experience revealed to me that the United States lags behind many other countries when it comes to options offered as part of paid leave policies.

My husband and I started discussing our options for our one-year-old child. One of the first things we did was spend time clarifying our values. When deciding who should take care of our son, my husband and I talked about our parenting and childcare priorities. We decided to divide the childcare responsibilities. Since I had stayed at home the first year in Germany, we decided my husband should stay home for the second year in the United States. This plan allowed us to achieve alignment and understand why we would both sacrifice a year of our career to care for our son.

I made the decision to leave my corporate job to start my company, LeaveLogic, focused on helping parents plan parental leave. This decision involved new challenges. I needed help to cope with changing my identity to one required of a successful entrepreneur. I sought the advice of a career coach to help me clarify the purpose of the business I wanted to start. Before becoming an entrepreneur, my identity was completely defined by my career path and future development plan as a corporate employee. Creating and running my own business was more complicated than my corporate job had been. My coach helped me realize the reasons why I was creating LeaveLogic. I constantly questioned if I should be a CEO and founder of a company. I had to embrace all of these various self-identities at the same time with lightning speed. Having a clear sense of purpose helped me do this.

After leaving my corporate job, I knew I needed to strengthen my support network. I was surprised at how difficult it was to find stories about people who had taken time out of their careers to be with their children and successfully returned to their careers. Slowly, I was able to find men and women who had made these choices in their lives and who were willing to talk with me. I asked these individuals questions about regrets or mistakes, and surprisingly I wasn't able to find anyone who said that they wished they hadn't taken time off to spend with their children. Many said it was the best career move that they had made. These conversations gave me the confidence to know that it was going to be all right. Ultimately, by strengthening my support network I was able to embark on my journey into entrepreneurship with an open heart.

One individual in my support network helped me gain clarity about my new business. I was introduced to an extremely talented user experience (UX) designer who owned his boutique UX design firm. He and his partner had consciously decided not to have any children, and didn't understand the mission of my new business. Unexpectedly, by working with him, I realized I was approaching LeaveLogic with a skewed perspective. For example, I didn't realize the varying costs of health care for pregnancy-related expenses. Having an objective person suggesting that I conduct customer interviews helped me uncover the importance of helping individuals understand health care costs. Ultimately, we were able to produce better software by interviewing our users instead of building what I thought was right.

When I first made the decision to leave my corporate job and create my company, I didn't feel a need to focus on self-care activities. However, an experience unfolded that helped me achieve a spiritual awakening. During the early days of creating my company, my family hosted an exchange student from Mexico. His parents had only one request. They wanted us to take him to Catholic Mass once a week, which I welcomed. I converted to Catholicism when I was twelve years old but hadn't been to Mass in over fifteen years. As I listened to the messages during these services, it started resonating with me and led to a spiritual awakening. I found a different kind of connectedness with the church than I'd had before. Several readings contained messages about forgiveness and the importance of letting go of perfection. These passages spoke to me about my journey of entrepreneurship. The more I believed and trusted that I was on the right path, the more courage I had to continue my journey. I found it was important for me to make time weekly for silent meditative introspection. I made time to reflect on what was bothering me as well as gratitude for my successes.

I learned many things about resiliency and thriving when I left my corporate job and started my company. I was determined to not just survive but thrive. I continue to learn more about resiliency every day and have summarized my advice for anyone embarking on a similar journey.

- Be prepared to surrender your control and become vulnerable. Building a company while having an infant and toddler meant I couldn't do it alone. I had to modify my expectations of what it meant to have a perfect house, spouse, and dinner. I became skilled at asking for help. Surrendering to different standards allowed me to make good decisions about running my business.

- Remember that life is short, and don't overlook people you care about. Many of the images we have of entrepreneurship are of twenty-four-hour workdays. I decided that life is too short for me to miss out on opportunities with my family. I challenged myself to build my company culture in a balanced way. I'm constantly asking myself, "Will the world end if I don't do this one thing today versus tomorrow?"

- Become more centered. Based on my work with my coach, I was able to create routines to center myself before speaking events or high-risk presentations. We did this by creating images and breathing routines which allow me to access an inner strength. For example, images that help me become centered and motivated include mothers saying goodbye to their children as they leave for work. This centering activity motivates me to keep finding choices for families.

- Be okay with people telling you that your idea won't work. Early in launching my business, I worked with an expert mentor. I initially believed that the mentor had all the answers, and if I followed his advice, everything would be fine. It took me a while to realize that my mentor's advice was just that, advice. This lesson taught me that it is all right to filter and prioritize advice. This insight gave me the courage to trust my wisdom to listen, but not always act.

- Give yourself permission to slow down. By slowing down, you allow the universe to interact with your actions versus obsessing about your agenda. One of the hardest things I found in retraining my corporate brain was surrendering and dancing with the universe, instead of feeling like I had to control everything that happened. I've learned to pause and reflect, acknowledging that there are certain forces outside of my control. As a result, this has helped me to become a much more effective entrepreneur and leader.

Biography

Anna Steffeney is the founder and CEO of LeaveLogic. LeaveLogic is a parental leave management platform, helping companies retain their top talent. In her free time Anna loves to spend time traveling with her family to visit family and friends around the world. You can find out more about LeaveLogic at www.LeaveLogic.com.

FOUR

RESILIENCY STRATEGY: STRENGTHEN SUPPORT NETWORKS

Proactively increase the depth and breadth of your support networks to help you maintain or regain balance in the midst of adversity.

Trapeze flyers are able to take daring risks because they know a net will catch them when they fall. A support network functions in similar ways as a psychological safety net-- enabling us to take huge leaps knowing it is there to catch us when we fail.
— Kevin Nourse

STRENGTHEN SUPPORT NETWORKS: MARTI'S STORY

Marti, a social media expert, transitioned into a new organization with hopes of creating more balance in her life to give her more time with the people she cared about most, but instead faced significant career adversity that nearly derailed her. After ten years in a large multinational Fortune

500 company, she grew tired of the nonstop travel and long hours. Most weeks she traveled 80 percent of the time, and as a result, her quality of life suffered. Many of her friends stopped calling, so when she came home from her travels, she often spent weekends at home without talking with anyone. Marti decided she needed to make a change and decided to explore job options in organizations that were smaller and slower-paced. After checking the online classified advertisements, she found her new employer. The organization she joined was a professional association that was woefully behind in establishing an online presence. She accepted the position, enthusiastic about the prospect of introducing new technologies to the association and how her life would positively change as a result of having more time for her friends and passions beyond work.

The euphoria she experienced in changing jobs quickly evaporated as problems began to surface. The contrast in organizational cultures between her former and current employer could not have been more striking. Marti's direct and task-oriented style, well-suited for her last organization, was not well received by her peers. In one particular meeting, while presenting her social media strategy to colleagues from across the organization, she responded impatiently to initial questions that she felt were so elementary. As a result, the rest of the meeting was largely silent. Her boss was in the room and looked particularly surprised and frustrated. Marti's spiral downward continued as a result of subsequent meetings that took on the same tone because of her style and lack of awareness of organizational cultural norms. For example, to get input from board members on certain social media platform approaches, she initiated a conference call without consulting her manager or the executive director. Her manager subsequently canceled the meeting and scolded Marti about her lack of awareness about the norms associated with board member interactions. Her manager explained that only the executive director was allowed to initiate these interactions. Marti felt embarrassed, angry, and frustrated. In her former organization, she had been expected to take bold action and interact with others regardless of organizational position or rank. Several colleagues who were frustrated by Marti's interpersonal style complained to her boss about her behavior and the way in which she implemented the social media strategy.

The stress Marti was experiencing in her new job stymied her intent to rebuild her personal relationships beyond her organization and establish more balance. At the end of the day, she would leave exhausted, eat a quick dinner, watch some television, and return to her computer to work a couple more hours. The few times she remembered her desire to reconnect with important people in her life resulted in periods of feeling guilty, but little outward action. Because she felt so embarrassed by all that had unfolded, she was reluctant to share her deepest concerns with her closest friends. Her lack of energy and motivation prevented her taking concrete actions to broaden her support network.

Marti persevered to achieve her professional goals, but began to regret her decision to join the organization. She felt like an impostor and began to worry that others would realize that she was not as talented as she appeared. She doubted her abilities to move forward with the social media strategy and began to make fun of her abilities in meetings, particularly when her manager was in the room. She often ate lunch alone, since her attempts to develop friendships with her colleagues were ignored. The stress of her work life, combined with few quality interactions with friends outside of work, began to weigh upon her. She worried a lot about her career and financial stability, fearful of losing her job. Marti reached out to her old boss with hopes of exploring the possibility of returning to her former position. Unfortunately, the position had already been filled, and her replacement was working out very well. She felt trapped and without options, longing for connection with supportive friends and professional colleagues who could help her get some perspective on the challenges she faced.

After three months in her new role without making much progress,

Marti received an unexpected email invitation to meet with her manager. She immediately felt stressed and on edge, fearing that she would be fired. During the meeting, her normally pleasant and upbeat manager was direct and to the point. Her manager explained how Marti's abrasive interpersonal style and lack of awareness of organizational cultural norms had damaged her reputation with her peers, the executive director, and even the association's board members. Marti would be fired if there were no improvements in her performance. Her manager helped her realize that her ideas for social media were excellent and very much on target for helping the association improve its interactions with members, but her interactions with others needed to improve substantially.

DERAILMENT TRIGGERS

Marti's story contains several triggers that contributed to her decline and near derailment:

1. **Lack of depth in a support network.**
   Marti lacked depth in her personal support network in terms of close, caring relationships with trusted allies who could empathize with her struggles. As a result, she constantly felt stressed and anxious. The isolation deepened her anxiety, creating a dysfunctional cycle of isolation and stress.

2. **Lack of breadth in a support network.**
   Marti lacked breadth in her support network of connections with people in her personal life, as well as other areas beyond her organization. This lack of breadth limited her effectiveness, since she had little awareness of the professional and industry-specific trends derived from supportive relationships in her profession and industry. In addition, this set her up for significant career adversity if she lost her job and the relatively few connections she had internal to her organization.

3. **Self-doubt and feeling like an impostor.**

   Marti's attempts at humor underscored a bigger issue she faced in her personal and professional life. She often felt like an impostor who had fooled everyone into believing she was competent. Because Marti held the core belief that everyone would eventually discover she was a fraud, she felt constant pressure to prove herself. Her attempt to build relationships by sarcastically belittling herself through humor backfired.

4. **Lack of alignment with her manager.**

   Another trigger was Marti's lack of alignment with her manager. In most cases, the relationship between an employee and their manager is the most critical relationship. Marti neglected to build a trusting relationship with her manager and, as a result, her manager was unwilling or unable to be an advocate for her in the organization.

DERAILMENT TRIGGER QUESTIONS

In light of the derailment triggers identified in Marti's story, there are several useful questions to ask yourself:

- Does my personal and professional support network have depth in terms of close, trusting relationships with people with whom I can share my fears and dreams?

- Does my support network have breadth, consisting of a variety of supportive relationships in different domains beyond my current organization?

- To what extent do I see myself as competent and effective? Does my behavior reflect my self-belief?

- How strong is the relationship I have with my manager? To what extent am I aligned with my manager on key outcomes for my role as well as strategies for meeting my goals?

By asking yourself these questions in advance of making a career change like Marti, you can anticipate potential challenges and maintain your resiliency.

DEFINING 'STRENGTHEN SUPPORT NETWORKS'

Support networks consist of personal and professional connections from which you draw support when faced with adversity and stress. Networks that are deep and broad are essential for helping you maintain stability in times of change and adversity, as well as helping you minimize or avoid adversity. The people in your support network, especially personal sources of support, often initially help you manage the emotions you may experience during tough times through caring and empathic emotional support. Subsequently, your support network can then help you take action to address your challenges by helping you create an action plan or holding you accountable for taking bold steps to enact it.

In addition to helping you cope effectively when you are faced with career adversity, support networks can help you anticipate adversity and prepare for it. For example, some of the ways that resilient people tap their support networks to prevent career adversity and thrive include:

- Learning about their strengths and weaknesses.

- Discovering how they are perceived in their organizations.

- Uncovering career opportunities and career traps.

- Brainstorming ways to handle challenging situations that, if not handled correctly, could lead to career-limiting mistakes.

Given that it takes time to develop trusting support networks, it is critical to establish and maintain support networks before you encounter career adversity. By proactively creating and maintaining your networks, you can be assured that your safety net is ready if you experience challenges in your career.

Your support networks should be deep, broad, current, and reciprocal. Depth consists of a range of closeness with others, from acquaintances to close confidants you can tap for emotional support. Resilient people typically have varying levels of depth in their network of relationships. However, given the amount of energy it takes to develop and sustain close supportive relationships, it is important to have a range of people in your support network. A network with breadth consists of substantive relationships from a variety of areas, not just your organization. It also includes your profession, your personal life, and your industry. People who unexpectedly lose their jobs often struggle because most of the people in their network work for the same organization. As a result, they may lose these trusted colleagues at the time they most need their support. A support network that is current means that you have stayed in touch with them to maintain your relationships through regular investments of time and attention. Beyond simply getting your needs met, well-designed support networks consist of two-way interactions. You must look out for their needs as well. In fact, the American Institute of Stress suggests that providing emotional support to others has the effect of helping the provider feel supported. You will feel better when you care for and support others.

Support comes in different forms. Highly resilient people are clear about the type and timing of the support they need. Therefore, the clearer you are about the support you need from others, the more likely you are to receive it. The table below summarizes specific types of support.

TYPE OF SUPPORT	DESCRIPTION
CHALLENGE	Feedback from others that prompts you to take action, such as observations about challenges you are experiencing, as well as perspectives on your strengths and weaknesses.

TYPE OF SUPPORT	DESCRIPTION
EMOTIONAL	Active listening, empathy, and understanding from another; a trusting and caring relationship with another that enables you to show your vulnerabilities.
INFORMATIONAL	Information from another about a challenge you are facing, such as actions you might take, options to consider, or potential roadblocks you might face.
INSTRUMENTAL	Resources shared by a supporter with you, such as tools, reference information, or access to key people.
MENTORING	Ongoing relationship with another to support your development; mentoring support usually involves a deeper level of trust and openness.
ROLE MODELLING	Nonverbal modeling of effective behavior by another who has faced a similar challenge.

STRENGTHEN SUPPORT NETWORKS ACTION STEPS

There are five action steps within *Strengthen Support Networks* that can be taken to help you proactively increase the breadth and depth of your support networks to help you maintain or regain balance in the midst of adversity:

1. Determine the kind of support you need.

2. Assess the quality of your support network.

3. Deepen your relationship with people in your network.

4. Maintain your professional network on a regular basis.

5. Identify ways to broaden your network.

Based on your assessment of your current support network in Action Step 1 and your support needs in Action Step 2, you may be in one of four situations, as summarized in the table below:

SCENARIO	RECOMMENDED ACTION STEPS
Support network has both breadth and depth	Action Step 4 to sustain your network
Support network is nonexistent	Reach out to people you identified in Action Step 1 that you may have lost contact with, then consider Action Step 5 to broaden your network
Support network has a depth of relationships but lacks breadth	Action Step 5 to broaden your network to multiple areas
Support network has a breadth of relationships but lacks depth	Action Step 3 and 4 to deepen the existing relationships in your network

You should use the Resiliency Action Plan to strengthen your support networks. By improving the breadth and depth of your safety net, you will be more successful in navigating current challenges you face as well as ensuring you are resilient in the midst of future adversity.

Stories abound of highly successful women who navigated substantial adversity in their careers and thrived, partly as a result of strong professional networks. Kelsey Ramsden was chosen as Canada's top female entrepreneur in 2012 and 2013 based on her experiences launching four successful businesses while coping with an ovarian cancer diagnosis. At 39 years old, she received global fame for her achievements. Yet, despite all her eventual success, Ramsden struggled with reinventing herself beyond her position as a management consultant, a role she grew to dread. She wrote, "Truth be told, it was less difficult getting others to respect and view me as competent and capable in my reinvented role than it was getting my own head around it. That's because I had valued myself according to how I had identified myself." As noted in *Forbes*, Ramsden spoke about the importance of support in establishing accountability with mentors and peers. She also underscored the importance of surrounding herself with people smarter than her and asking for help. Beyond simply exchanging business cards with people, the key is "looking at all connections as a living thing—maintain and deepen them with every contact." She described how important it was for her to find a "reinvention mentor" who she could tap to help her understand how to transition into a new professional identity as well as model the behavior she needed to embrace.

STRENGTHEN SUPPORT NETWORKS: MARTI'S RESILIENCY ACTION PLAN

After leaving the meeting with her manager, Marti felt a range of emotions. While she felt some relief in learning what the issue was, her most pervasive feeling was pain and embarrassment for not realizing how she was coming across to others, as well as the impact it could have on her career. Marti ruminated on situations in the past few months where she obviously missed some important social clues in her interactions on the job. Marti felt alone, isolated, and unsure of her next steps.

After thinking about the situation she faced for several days, Marti knew she needed to take action to find emotional support and identify a plan to move forward. In assessing her support network, she recalled several people she used to be very close to but lost touch with. Marti took a risk and reached out to a former graduate school friend she was very close to. Her former friend was elated to hear from her. They met for dinner, and after a few minutes catching up, the emotional dam broke as Marti tearfully shared many of the overwhelming feelings associated with her work situation. After listening to her story and empathizing with her based on some career struggles she had experienced, Marti's friend shared the name of a career coach she worked with that made a big impact in her own career. Marti had no idea her friend had also experienced some tough career challenges. She instantly felt more hopeful as a result of the meeting, apologized for losing touch with her friend, and committed to staying in closer touch. The validation and support she received completely shifted her perspective, gave her more hope, and helped her become more receptive to taking action.

In the weeks after that dinner meeting, Marti reached out to the career coach and began to improve the navigation of the situation. After meeting with the coach two times, she developed an action plan to help her move forward that included:

- Strategies for ensuring she had enough personal support.

- Identifying other types of support she might need in her journey to recover from her career struggles.

- Clarifying ways she could deepen her relationship with people in her support network.

- Ways to improve the relationship with her manager to assure support for her role as well as receive regular feedback.

- Setting up a schedule of regular ongoing meetings to deepen relationships with internal contacts, learn about their concerns, and gather input for her social media plans for the association.

- Identifying and exploring professional and industry associations to broaden her network.

Once Marti finalized her plan, she moved into action quickly. She initially reached out to other personal friends she had long lost contact with and scheduled time to reconnect. Marti also met with her manager and shared her action plan, along with inviting ongoing feedback about her efforts to rebuild key relationships in the organization. She asked her manager to observe her in meetings in her attempts to soften her approach and provide positive or developmental feedback. Next, as a result of completing an assessment of her support network, she realized how few people she knew outside her organization. She immediately joined the American Society of Association Executives (ASAE) and began exploring the possibility of working on a committee. Marti also identified a finance manager in her organization who could serve as a potential mentor for her in navigating the organizational culture. One reason Marti chose her is that this manager had such a different personality style and could help her find new ways to communicate and gain support for her ideas. Marti then worked through her list of organizational stakeholders and conducted short meetings to better understand their functional areas and concerns about her social media plans.

Two months after Marti received the disturbing feedback from her manager, she began to notice progress. She made a point to reconnect and deepen the relationship with her graduate school friend and others she had lost contact with. This group of people was emerging as a key component in her support network as they shared stories of their hopes and challenges. She made these gatherings a priority on her calendar. In her regular meetings with key stakeholders, several began to speak more transparently about their concerns associated with her proposed social media strategies. As a result, she was able to incorporate their ideas into her strategies. The feedback she was receiving from her manager and her mentor was helping her adapt her style to be less confrontational and more relaxed in her interactions with others, thereby building support for her strategy. Marti began balancing her need for support from others with offers to help some of the people in her network. She no longer felt guilty about asking for support, and others seemed to appreciate how she was looking out for them. Though she still had much work to do, she felt much more grounded and optimistic for the future, thanks in large part to the actions she took to rebuild her safety net.

STRENGTHEN SUPPORT NETWORKS: RESILIENCY ACTION PLAN ACTIVITIES

The purpose of this strategy is to help you proactively increase the breadth and depth of your support networks to help you maintain or regain balance in the midst of adversity. There are five actions that you can take to help strengthen your support networks:

1. Determine the kind of support you need.

2. Assess the quality of your support network.

3. Identify ways to deepen your support network.

4. Engage your support network on a regular basis.

5. Identify ways to broaden your support network.

The following five activities will help you take action to strengthen your support networks. For each of these activities, you will be invited to capture a key outcome as well as a SMART goal in the Resiliency Action Plan Summary Worksheet at the end of this chapter.

ACTIVITY 1: DETERMINE THE KIND OF SUPPORT YOU NEED

This activity is designed to help you determine the types of support you might need to address an issue, challenge, or development goal. By determining the type of support you need, you will be better prepared to enlist the help of others in attaining this support. In addition to eliciting support from people in your support network, you may need to look to professionals such as coaches or therapists. In activity two, you will have an opportunity to revisit your needs to identify potential sources.

INSTRUCTIONS

1. Reflect on your challenges or development goals and refer to the Support Needed Assessment worksheet (**Table 4.1**):

a. Identify your issue, challenge, or development goal.

b. Determine the types of support you need to address your issue, challenge, or development goal.

c. Identify the timing of the support you need (e.g., a specific date or a regular time interval such as monthly).

d. Identify some thoughts on the impact of receiving this type of support on your ability to respond to the issue, challenge, or development goal.

e. Leave the "sources" field blank for now. You will revisit this after you complete Activity 2.

Table 4.1

Support Needed Assessment Worksheet				
Challenge/Goal	Type	Timing	Impact	Sources

 Refer to the Resiliency Action Plan Summary Worksheet (**Table 4.5**) at the end of this chapter and capture your critical support needs.

ACTIVITY 2: ASSESS THE QUALITY OF YOUR NETWORK

The purpose of this activity is to provide a starting point for strengthening your support network by creating an inventory of individuals with whom you are connected. This activity will help you identify any gaps in your network. With this knowledge, you can then take action to fill these gaps and ensure that your professional network has both breadth and depth.

INSTRUCTIONS

1. Refer to the Support Network Assessment worksheet (**Table 4.2**) and identify the people in your network, starting first with your

personal connections, and then your current organization, your
profession, your sector, and then other contacts that do not fit in
other categories. Consider identifying people you are currently
interacting with and those you may have lost touch with. Consider
each of the following fields for each person in your network:

a. Name

b. Status of the relationship in terms of closeness:

  - Level 1: You have been introduced.

  - Level 2: You have basic knowledge of each other.

  - Level 3: You have a trusting relationship.

  - Level 4: This person is a very close contact or confidant;
    you can share confidential information about yourself
    with this person.

c. Interests/Needs: Identify this person's interests, needs, or
challenges.

d. Last Contact Date: Note when you last interacted with this
person.

Table 4.2

Support Network Assessment Worksheet					
Category		Name	Status	Interests	Last Contact
Personal	Friends				
	Family				
	Community				
	Other				
Organization	Your Boss				
	Subordinates				
	Peers				
	Others				
Profession					
Industry					
Other					

2. Once you complete this inventory, reflect on the following questions:

    a. What do you notice about your network in terms of breadth (number of contacts in each category) and depth (range of levels of connectedness)?

    b. Which category of your network is the strongest and which is the weakest in terms of number of contacts or depth of connection?

    c. Where do you need to focus your relationship-building activities based on this analysis?

    d. Are there any people in your network you have lost touch with that could be excellent sources of support if you rekindled the relationship?

3. Revisit the list of support needs you identified in Activity 1. Based on this assessment, who could be potential sources of support for each of the challenges or goals you identified? Refer to the sources column. (**Table 4.1**)

 Refer to the Resiliency Action Plan Summary Worksheet (**Table 4.5**) at the end of this chapter and identify a SMART goal associated with actions you could take to engage potential sources of support. For example: *Reach out to X by September 30 to gain insights on strategies she uses to effectively integrate her work and life.*

ACTIVITY 3: IDENTIFY WAYS TO DEEPEN YOUR SUPPORT NETWORK
One of the best ways to ensure you have a strong, robust support network is to look out for others and provide support where possible. Doing so can have a positive impact on your reputation and deepen the emotional connection you have with others. Looking out for others' interests will be particularly critical when you face situations where you need to enlist their support in the future.

INSTRUCTIONS

1. Refer to the Support Network Assessment worksheet (**Table 4.2**) in Activity 2 and identify five contacts you most want to deepen your relationship with.

2. Review the interests/needs you identified for each of them.

3. For each contact, identify two ways you can help them, such as:
    *   Share information that may help them navigate a challenge.
    *   Make an introduction for them.
    *   Speak positively on their behalf to others.
    *   Refer business leads or other opportunities to them.
    *   Arrange a lunch or phone call to learn more about their needs and ways you can help.

4. Identify the approach you will take for each of your five contacts on the following worksheet. (**Table 4.3**)

Table 4.3

Deepen Your Support Worksheet		
Contact	**Needs or Interests**	**Strategies to Deepen the Relationship**

 Refer to the Resiliency Action Plan Summary Worksheet (**Table 4.5**) at the end of this chapter and identify a SMART goal associated with deepening your support network. For example: *Email a relevant article to five colleagues that I most want to deepen the relationship with by October 15.*

ACTIVITY 4: ENGAGE YOUR SUPPORT NETWORK
ON A REGULAR BASIS

A professional network is a living entity that needs regular time and attention to ensure it remains current. Many people are great at establishing connections, but not very effective in maintaining these relationships. This activity will focus on maintaining the viability and currency of your professional network so that it is ready and available if you should need to draw upon others for a challenge.

INSTRUCTIONS

1. Refer to the Support Network Assessment worksheet in Activity 2 (**Table 4.2**) and identify two contacts in each category where the last contact date is the least current.

2. For each contact, identify the best way to engage them:
    *   Email update with some recent news.
    *   Phone call.
    *   Lunch date.
    *   Written card.

 Refer to the Resiliency Action Plan Summary Worksheet (**Table 4.5**) at the end of this chapter and identify a SMART goal to engage your support network more regularly. For example: *On the first day of each month, schedule a lunch meeting with one of my ten most critical professional colleagues.*

ACTIVITY 5: IDENTIFY WAYS TO BROADEN
YOUR SUPPORT NETWORK

By far, one of the best ways to build a professional support network is involvement in professional, trade, and alumni associations. Joining an association is a relatively low-cost way to have access to some types of support, including:

- Meetings and conferences to network with other professionals.

- Formal mentoring and development programs at low or no cost.

- Information about emerging trends in the profession or industry, as well as best practice information.

- Online resources and communities.

- Career resources, such as job banks and position-referral services.

- Opportunities to develop leadership skills.

Most associations offer both local chapters in your community as well as national organizations to increase the breadth of your professional networks.

INSTRUCTIONS

1. Identify potential associations using the following strategies:
   a. Engage others in your profession for their advice on the appropriate associations to join.
   b. Access the site www.careeronestop.org to search for American professional associations you can join.
   c. Search the Internet using the phrase "international association" for a list of global associations that you may consider affiliating with.

2. For each association that appears to be relevant to your needs, capture the following in the worksheet (**Table 4.4**):
   a. Name of the association.
   b. Professional or industry focus.
   c. Type of association.
      - Local association that has meetings in your geographic

area which you can attend.

- National association that conducts large conferences annually.

  d. A summary of the member benefits available to you.
  e. The cost of membership.

Table 4.4

Broadening Your Network Worksheet					
Association Name	Focus	Type	Member Benefits	Cost	Status
Professional Associations					
Trade or Industry Associations					
Alumni Associations					

3. Once you capture a working list of potential associations, follow up with each of them to clarify their suitability for your role. Indicate the status of your follow-up with each (e.g., open or closed).

 Refer to the Resiliency Action Plan Summary Worksheet (**Table 4.5**) at the end of this chapter and identify a SMART goal to increase the breadth of your network. For example: *By November 7 I will attend a meeting of one professional association and introduce myself to the membership chairperson.*

RESILIENCY ACTION PLAN SUMMARY WORKSHEET
Refer to the worksheet (**Table 4.5**) to summarize key outcomes and SMART goals from the activities in this chapter.

For each activity associated with this strategy, make sure you have identified a key outcome or SMART goal to help you take action. Capture these commitments in your day planner or calendar to ensure that you complete them.

Table 4.5

✓	Resiliency Action Plan Summary Worksheet
Activity	**Key Outcome or SMART Goals**
1	
2	
3	
4	
5	

ADDITIONAL RESOURCES

The following resources consist of online videos, apps, and assessment tools that may give you greater depth on key concepts associated with this Resiliency Strategy. We have no control over and do not endorse third-party content, goods, or services.

- 7 Tips for Effective Networking (Video, 9 minutes). Available at https://youtu.be/JY-PEvX4ySs.

- Namerick (App). Useful tool for helping you remember a person's name and details after you meet them. Available at http://namerick.com.

- Professional Networking Rules (Video, 4 minutes). Available at https://youtu.be/NLLevUjoyvg.

- Professional networking in the modern workplace—EY in collaboration with Julia Hobsbawm (Video, 3 minutes). Available at https://youtu.be/kdRt0ckVl9M.

- Shapr (App). Enables you to find other professionals based on interests. Available at http://www.shapr.net.

FIVE

SANDY'S STORY: TRUSTING MY WINGS AS I LEARN TO FLY, AGAIN

BY SANDY SWANTON

The challenge is to design your life as you would a strategy for a client. Design it, negotiate the stuff, and dance through the minefield of ambitions and reality.
— CATHERINE TOWNSEND

I was in my late thirties when I first became a victim of workplace bullying. As a communications professional, resolving challenges to find solutions had always been a core skill. While improving my skills through education and experience had served me well, few programs or companies teach you how to work with bullies. I had returned home to Australia after living and working in western Canada for eleven years. The decision to move back to Australia answered many personal and professional goals. All I had to do was find a way to work through the culture shock of reintegrating into society and a workforce that didn't easily welcome expatriates returning home after a long stay in another country.

With courage, stubbornness, and the will to make things work, I stayed in Australia almost ten years. I spent time with my aging parents, completed graduate studies, worked with some fabulous people, and moved my career forward into government communications. It was during my years in Australia that I experienced workplace bullying in two different organizations. The second experience triggered my move back to Canada after reflecting on the decision for seven weeks. While many in my life considered this move rash, it was a relief to be heading back to my second home, a country where I hadn't experienced workplace bullying before.

Workplace bullying looks different in every situation. Each time I was the target of bullies, they used a slightly different combination of behaviors. I've experienced bullies gatekeeping important information, criticizing new approaches I suggested, undermining my credibility, and physically trying to intimidate me with aggressive behavior. In each case, the bullies were not my direct supervisor and did not know my job or professional background. In fact, they had no intention of understanding my role or demands and had a history of attacking staff in this way.

When I returned to Canada, I continued to work in senior communications positions. After three years, I was recruited into a new role within a strong and growing team. Excited about the opportunity and optimistic for the future, I tackled the required relocation with a now well-practiced transition strategy and moved back to a favorite city. Sadly, within the first two months it became apparent that a senior team member had well-known, but undocumented, bullying behaviors. Among the staff across the organization that knew about this bully was the human resources director, who did not acknowledge the situation. Proposing new methods or offering different opinions triggered the bullying behavior. The behaviors I experienced included vindictive gossip, physical intimidation, and reputation sabotage.

Unwilling to tolerate the unhealthy behaviors, I approached human resources. Human resources told me that they welcomed the opportunity to support a staff member prepared to take on the challenge of documenting the situation. They also indicated that they preferred to have more than one staff member come forward. Choosing my timing and words carefully, I spoke with select colleagues. It quickly became apparent why there was nothing on record about the bullying. No one was prepared to risk talking about the behaviors for fear of being labelled as a troublemaker, or worse, as incompetent. Neither label was fair, but the fear was very real, and no one would come forward with me.

Feeling isolated and concerned about my future work and happiness, I began considering my future. After such a hopeful start, everything had changed. Because I was experienced at adjusting my hopes and expectations, I consciously set about reviewing what had happened, and started looking for ways forward. I realized that I would go into this alone, as I had in the past. This time I felt the need to make a big change beyond a geographic change and discover if I still had the wings to fly in a new direction. I chose to move from the experience of being bullied to considering options for my future, within a very short period of time. As a three-time expatriate, I knew I had personal strengths and strategies to guide me forward. In the safety of my home, I was able to explore the unhealthy work situation I had experienced. I became more self-aware and was better able to understand the situation and consider my role. As a result, I distinguished what I was responsible for from the behaviors of others.

As I explored my stress level, I recalled that taking care of me was my first priority. Despite still experiencing negativity at work, I took action to regain my physical and emotional balance. I reviewed my options for support, and to my great relief, discovered friends in unusual places. To gain clarity about the situation, I engaged my director in a nonconfrontational discussion to determine if a change was possible. Unfortunately, the director determined that the bullying episode was nothing more than a difference of personalities. I was relieved to learn that she wanted to support me and no longer questioned my legitimacy on the team.

With the immediate crisis over, I focused on clarifying my purpose. I asked myself if I should continue on my current career path. While I loved the work, I was now physically and emotionally tired of constantly being under attack by colleagues. I knew it was time to make the decision to leave or commit to staying for another decade. Over a five-week period I reviewed my values, passions, and vision for the future. Using Post-It notes spread across my large dining table with one concept per note, I examined where I wanted to live and work. Travel was one of my core values and a passion. I looked at all my options from different directions and asked myself tough questions.

I asked for the support of good friends who knew me well and brainstormed other aspects of my values and passions with them. I subsequently created new Post-It notes, edited existing notes, and reorganized the themes that emerged. With the Post-It notes spread before me, I was able to let the information from the process sink in and identify the deeper meaning. I considered all my options and reflected on the possibilities for a few days. Through all of this, I continued to work long hours, took care of myself, and leaned on others when needed. As a new vision for my future started to appear, I gained a renewed sense of energy both for the job at hand and my life. I did indeed still have wings, but wondered if I could still fly.

After a period, I decided to share my new vision with two people who knew me well. I explained my desire for a more sustainable future that nurtured my core with less negativity and upheaval. I explained the research I had done to arrive at this new vision. In each case, their support and feedback came in the form of questions, which we worked through over a few days. The process was initially slow, but once started, it flowed easily in powerful discussions. What had been roadblocks became the starting point for research, leading to additional options and more research. I needed to feel comfortable that my wings would support my flight in this new direction.

Moving between countries, working with small and large organizations, and having opportunities to learn, lead, and mentor were valuable parts of my career journey. But after more than twenty-five years in the communications field, I realized I'd had enough. If I was going to thrive, not just survive, I needed to move on. My experiences helped me realize that I have the power to decide how long I want to fight my battles. This process showed me that I did not want to dance through this minefield of negativity and burnout anymore. I decided to take a different path.

The next phase of my transition involved a geographic and career change. I moved to Florence, Italy. I love the country and the organic nature of the city, the culture, the people, the food, and the completely different pace of life. I took a course to learn to teach English. I teach business English online using technology to work with my adult students all over the world as they strive for their goals. I am slowly learning Italian. While I gave up my comfortable salary and lifestyle, I gained so much, including the realization that I am much better at quickly seeing what is mine to change.

Almost a decade before I moved to Italy, I worked at a professional organization in Australia. One late October evening, the local chapter held a women's forum titled "Perceptions of Success," and I recently found the notes I took that night. Each of the panel members, highly qualified professionals in their own right, spoke calmly, passionately, and positively about the choices we can make, if only we choose to be bold. We get to choose what success looks like to us. It is not someone else's decision, unless we give them that authority. Accepting ourselves, looking after ourselves, and choosing to be confident about all that we have makes each of us a better person for work and life. That is our choice and something I celebrate every day.

Over the past two years, my purpose has been clarified as I moved from corporate life and stepped off the ledge, found my wings, and remembered I could fly. I wouldn't have it any other way! This process has validated my strengths and helped me achieve a sense of calmness that others see too. I am better at choosing me. The following are my suggestions on how to be resilient and thrive.

- Choose to live and work intentionally, and to go back to the basics of you. I am developing my next career as a travel writer, photographer, and blogger. My stress level has significantly decreased, my life is simpler, and I enjoy my holidays from the second I leave my house.

No longer does it take a week or two to unwind from the stress of my job when I go on vacation. I no longer dread going home when my holiday is over and facing hundreds of work emails.

- Find your dream and do something about it. I've been told by many that my choice to try something new when doors seemed to be closing has inspired them to consider their choices. New opportunities are not only open to the young. Rather, they are open to everyone, if you are prepared to try. There is no expiration date for having a dream and doing something about it.

- Choose to be untethered to other people's expectations of the path you will follow. This is not always easy, but it does make for an interesting life. It also doesn't always mean moving around the world or even across the country. Sometimes it means making a plan for your future and slowly, quietly, taking the steps to make it happen. The people I meet in Italy remind me of that every day.

- Be patient with yourself, the time it takes to live a dream, and with others. A favorite quote from David G. Allen on my pin board reminds me every day, "Patience is the calm acceptance that things can happen in a different order than the one you have in mind." Some days it is good to be able to fly as I dance through the minefield of my new ambitious dreams and reality.

BIOGRAPHY

An international traveler since the age of 6, Sandy Swanton now combines her love of travel with a career of working with words and images as a travel writer and photographer, and business English teacher in Italy. In her free time, she travels even more—even just down the road, to meet new people and taste life, stepping out of the corporate world for the next chapters of her life. You can find out more about Sandy at globalwanderings.ca and reach her at sandy@globalwanderings.ca.

SIX

RESILIENCY STRATEGY: CLARIFY PURPOSE

*Focus on understanding your values, passions, vision, mission, and goals
to boost your sense of optimism, align your behavior, and take action.*

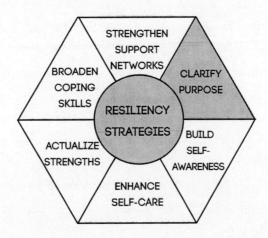

*Too much noise can cloud your senses. Stopping to listen to the silence can
help you gain perspective on what is really important.*
— Lynn Schmidt

CLARIFY PURPOSE: JANE'S STORY

Jane had the perfect career. She moved up the career ladder quickly. She
progressed rapidly through the ranks of every organization she worked
for, going from individual contributor to manager to director. Her
responsibilities continued to grow throughout her career. Others perceived
her as a high-potential employee. Jane's performance reviews were always

excellent, and her managers saw her as someone they could count on to get the job done.

After twenty years of working in similar industries, Jane made the decision to take a new job in an industry she hadn't worked in before. The culture of the organization was different. The organization moved at a slower pace with more bureaucracy. Her first year went well. Her responsibilities were similar to those she had excelled in previously, and she had a good relationship with her manager. As a next step in her career, Jane accepted a new position in the same organization. She would be working in a different department, leading an initiative that was outside her area of expertise. This new position would be a stretch assignment for her. The opportunity to grow her skills and lead a visible and important project for the organization excited her.

The job involved the implementation of new software. The position required Jane to work at a different facility in the same area, which increased her commute time from forty-five minutes to two hours each day. Jane began reporting to a different manager, and the role required her to expand her team from ten to thirty people. Initially the project went well. But as Jane's responsibilities grew and the project expanded, she began encountering issues with her new manager, project stakeholders, and team members.

As can often happen with the implementation of new software, there were multiple challenges. Not all project requirements were met, and some completion dates slipped. Jane's typically direct communication style and sense of urgency to drive results, which had worked for her in previous industries, did not go over as well in this new environment. In the midst of the project delays, her relationship with her new manager began to deteriorate, and Jane received negative feedback about her performance. Jane did not feel that her manager was supportive, and trust deteriorated. Communication between Jane and her manager began to break down. While Jane had not initially minded the additional commute time, she began to feel an impact on her family life and the time she had to spend with her children.

At the same time, key project stakeholders stopped responding to Jane's request for support. Some of the team members she had hired began complaining that Jane's leadership style was too demanding. At Jane's next performance review, she received a poor performance evaluation from her manager. She had been in the new role less than a year. Her manager removed her as a leader of the software implementation project and demoted her to a different role in the same department. Jane believed that she had become the scapegoat for project issues and that's why she had been demoted. Her dislike for her manager grew. She shared her perspective with others and developed an attitude regarded as negative by many.

After being on a fast track for twenty years, Jane experienced a devastating failure at work for the first time. Her new job hadn't worked out as she had expected. The large gap between her expectations and reality caused Jane significant unhappiness at work. This affected both her work life and personal life. Jane was stuck in a job she didn't want, and she didn't know how to get out. She wanted to move on, but she knew it would be difficult to leave her company and get a job elsewhere. So she stayed stuck, and her work situation continued to deteriorate. Jane's level of stress at work became high. Her unhappiness affected her behavior, the quality of her work, and her relationships with others. She was caught up in a vicious cycle that kept repeating itself, and she couldn't see a way out. As a result, Jane began to lose hope that anything could change and became increasingly angry. Several months after the demotion, Jane started working with a coach to help her turn the situation around.

DERAILMENT TRIGGERS

Jane's situation is not unique. It could happen to anyone. Jane made some significant career decisions without fully analyzing the possible impact of those decisions. She did not put plans in place to mitigate potential issues. Jane got excited about a new job opportunity and did not take the time to examine how the opportunity aligned with her values, passions, vision, and mission. Jane's career issues are common experiences in the workplace, where an organization's needs may not always align with a leader's career interests, skills, or leadership style. Had Jane taken time to step back and reflect on her situation, she would have identified at least four potential derailment triggers:

1. **A job in a new industry.**
   Jane accepted a job in an industry with a very different culture from what she was used to. It was a slower-moving organization, requiring more layers of approval and stakeholder involvement. Jane typically moved quickly to get things done, and she wasn't used to the levels of bureaucracy in this organization.

2. **A stretch assignment.**
   Jane took a stretch assignment to grow her skills and capabilities. That is a common way to develop and grow in organizations. What Jane didn't do is take time to assess her ability to do the new job. It is important to evaluate the skills required to be successful in a stretch assignment. Once the skills are identified, the next step is to determine the gap between current and desired skills and create an action plan to close that gap.

3. **A new manager.**
   Jane had many new managers as she progressed in her career. Since those relationships had worked in the past, she assumed that this relationship with a new manager would also be successful. As Jane's story highlights, that is not always the case. Taking the time to learn more about a new manager's expectations and clearly define goals can be a critical step in planning how to be successful in a new role.

4. **Work and life integration concerns.**

   Jane was excited about the stretch assignment and accepted the position without giving much thought to the effect the increased commute time would have on her personal life. As the job demands increased, the time Jane had to spend with her family decreased. She began to feel the effect of not having as much time to spend with her children, which increased her stress level.

Any one of these triggers can present significant challenges for an individual. The impact of the triggers grows tremendously when they occur simultaneously and without adequate support. When the demands of a job exceed the resources available, the result can be feelings of overwhelm, chronic stress, and burnout. It can become difficult to think clearly and strategically about problems at a time when it is most important to do so. That is why it is important to evaluate resiliency strategies proactively prior to accepting a new position. Here are some specific questions to consider for clarifying your purpose for each of the four derailment triggers.

DERAILMENT TRIGGER QUESTIONS

These questions will help you to clarify your purpose and navigate or avoid derailment. Ask yourself these questions prior to taking on a new position or assignment.

- Do the values of the people in the new industry align with your values?

- Are you passionate about the stretch assignment?

- Does the stretch assignment align with the values, vision, mission, and goals you have for your professional life?

- How does what you want to achieve align with the goals of your new manager?

- How will the increased commute time affect your work and life integration?

DEFINING 'CLARIFY PURPOSE'

Clarifying your purpose requires you to understand your values, passions, vision, mission, and goals to boost your sense of optimism, align your behavior, and take action. There are five key terms associated with *Clarify Purpose*.

- Values

- Passions

- Vision

- Mission

- Goals

Your values represent underlying beliefs that motivate action. Examples of values are creativity, achievement, health, joy, prosperity, security, and teamwork. Values are core beliefs that you need to act upon, or they are merely words on paper. They should be an integral part of your daily decision-making. In a perfect world, professional roles embody core values. For example, *Susan is a leader in information technology, and her values include achievement, innovation, service, health, and family.*

Your passions typically spring from your core values. As an example, *Susan has a passion for working at a nonprofit that focuses on eradicating cancer. This desire is anchored in her core values of achievement, innovation, service, health, and family.* Working in a position that does not align with your identified values and passions can lead to frustration and unhappiness. That is why achieving clarity on your values and passions is an important characteristic of resiliency. That clarity can help you thrive and grow when you face career challenges.

Your vision statement should be a compelling image of the future. It describes your desired future state, but not the action steps to get there. It is typically a one- or two-sentence statement and it aligns with your articulated values. An example of Susan's vision statement is, *I will be a leader in helping cancer researchers discover innovative cures for cancer. I will have loving relationships with my husband and children.*

Your mission statement focuses on how to accomplish the vision. It is typically a paragraph, four to five sentences, and is more focused on the broad activities necessary to achieve the vision. Mission statements address the questions of who, what, where, when, why, and how. Susan's example mission statement declares: *In my current role I will be a leader in information technology at a cancer research center. I will lead an innovative IT team focused on creating new software applications and data mining techniques for cancer researchers. Cancer researchers will be able to use the applications and techniques to uncover promising trends with new compounds that may cure cancer. My work and home life will be balanced in order to spend quality time with my family.*

Your goals are what enable you to accomplish your mission. Write your goals in a SMART format: S – specific, M – measurable, A – achievable, R – result-focused, and T – time-based. Using a SMART format to create your goals will help to ensure that you have created goals that you can accomplish. One of Susan's goals is, *Create two new job descriptions by the second quarter for my IT roles that include specifics on the skills required to innovatively create new software applications and data mining techniques for cancer researchers in order to hire the best talent.*

CLARIFY PURPOSE ACTION STEPS

There are five action steps within *Clarify Purpose* that can be taken to help determine your values, passions, vision, mission, and goals.

1. Identify the core values that make you unique.

2. Understand the passions and interests that motivate you.

3. Develop a clear sense of vision for your life and career.

4. Create a mission aligned with your values, passions, and vision.

5. Implement goals that enable you to accomplish your mission.

You can use the Resiliency Action Plan beforehand to create strategies for avoiding challenges or for thriving despite difficult situations. By clarifying your values, passions, vision, mission, and goals, you can make the best career choices in advance of making changes. Resiliency strategies also help you to maintain perspective in the midst of a significant challenge. Mika Brzezinski, cohost of MSNBC's *Morning Joe*, knew her values, passions, and vision at an early age, and this knowledge helped her stay on her desired path when faced with career challenges.

Mika's parents' own careers influenced her career choice, and she became a network news anchor. Shortly before Mika turned forty, she was fired from CBS News. It was a difficult experience for her. She described it as "going from everything to everyone to nothing to no one." She had difficulty getting another job as a news anchor, and her money began to dwindle. She interviewed for other types of jobs outside of her desired career path. She received a job offer for a position as a vice president at a public relations firm, and she declined it and referred a friend. Mika realized that even though she needed a job, there was only one career for her, the one she had chosen many years ago working for the news networks. Mika remained true to her vision and took a part-time job doing freelance work with MSNBC. After only a few months, she was moved into a full-time role as the host of a new morning show. Staying true to her values and vision paid off and helped her remain resilient in spite of the difficulties she encountered along the way.

Even individuals who have articulated their values, vision, and mission will still face unanticipated career challenges. When that happens, it's important to be able to revisit and recommit to the values, vision, and mission that you have established. You can use them as a guide to determine alignment and the best next steps.

CLARIFY PURPOSE: JANE'S RESILIENCY ACTION PLAN

The negative work experience severely shook Jane's confidence. She had never experienced a bad relationship with one of her managers or received a poor performance evaluation. She had always excelled at work. The demotion took an emotional and physical toll on her that she didn't realize until she began to have coaching discussions. She thought she could simply push through the emotional aspects of the failure. What Jane realized is that she couldn't discuss her feelings about the situation with anyone, including her husband. She was embarrassed and ashamed.

Over a three-month period Jane and her coach were able to build a trusting relationship in which Jane felt comfortable sharing her feelings. She acknowledged her feelings about the demotion. She disclosed how the experience had devastated her. She cried and released a flood of emotions that she had kept inside. The emotional breakthrough helped Jane identify her true values and create a plan with clear goals for next steps. The breakthrough enabled Jane to increase her resiliency and grow from the experience. To thrive, not just survive.

Jane worked with her coach to create an action plan to help her restore and increase her resiliency, as well as enable her to grow and thrive as she dealt with her career challenges. Jane's plan focused on clarifying her purpose:

- Getting clear on her values and what was important to her.

- Understanding what she was passionate about in her work and personal life.

- Creating her vision to align with her values and passions.

- Developing a mission statement that would help her achieve her vision of the type of career she wanted.

- Implementing goals focused on specific actions, such as networking, that would move Jane toward accomplishing her mission.

Jane's plan had numerous goals, both professional and personal. Her core values were happiness, family, self-improvement, learning, and being healthy. Her vision focused on achieving happiness and fulfillment in a new job that aligned with her passions. Her mission included getting a new job that enabled her to make the most of her skills and abilities and achieve work and life integration. Her goals were aligned to make this happen.

Jane continued to work on her action plan. Three months later she received an offer for a new job in the same organization, working for a different manager. Because of Jane's dedication to implementing her Resiliency Action Plan, others in the organization noticed a change in her behavior. Jane became more positive and influential as she clarified her values, vision, mission, and goals. She got a new job strongly aligned with her values and vision. The requirements of the job also aligned with Jane's passions and interests. Her commute time would be reduced, allowing her to achieve a better work and life integration. Jane accepted the job and thrived in the position, working with a new manager. She continued applying the skills she learned about resiliency in order to continue to grow and be successful.

By clarifying your purpose, you are taking steps to determine the values, passions, vision, mission, and goals that are critical for your success. In Jane's case, her focus on clarifying her purpose happened after the career derailment experience took place. The Resiliency Action Plan can be used proactively to create resiliency strategies to assist in avoiding career challenges and derailment experiences. By doing so, you can make the best career choices in advance of making changes.

CLARIFY PURPOSE: RESILIENCY ACTION PLAN ACTIVITIES

The purpose of this strategy is to help you understand your values, passions, vision, mission, and goals to boost your sense of optimism, align your behavior, and take action. There are five actions that you can take to help clarify your purpose.

1. Identify the core values that make you unique.

2. Understand the passions and interests that motivate you.

3. Develop a clear sense of vision for your life and career.

4. Create a mission aligned with your values, passions, and vision.

5. Implement goals that enable you to accomplish your mission.

The following five activities will help you take action to clarify your purpose.

ACTIVITY 1: IDENTIFY THE CORE VALUES THAT MAKE YOU UNIQUE

During this activity you reflect on your most recent experiences where you felt alive and engaged. You identify your passions and use the Core Values Worksheet (**Table 6.1**) to find your top five values. Identifying your top five values and passions enables you to create and align your vision and mission with your values and passions.

Instructions

1. Reflect on five peak experiences you have had in the past one to three years. These experiences are examples of instances or accomplishments where you felt alive, engaged, and focused. These experiences typically illustrate your passions and focus on interests that motivate you. You can draw from your personal or professional roles. Describe these experiences by writing each story and

highlighting the passions and interests illustrated in each experience.

- Experience 1:
- Experience 2:
- Experience 3:
- Experience 4:
- Experience 5:

Table 6.1

Core Values Worksheet											
Experiences					Core Value Present?	Experiences					Core Value Present?
1	2	3	4	5		1	2	3	4	5	
					Achievement						Joy
					Adventure						Justice
					Ambition						Leadership
					Appreciation						Love
					Authenticity						Optimism
					Beauty						Persistence
					Challenge						Pleasure
					Competence						Proactivity
					Confidence						Prosperity
					Control						Recognition
					Courage						Reflection
					Creativity						Reliability
					Education						Resiliency
					Endurance						Sacrifice
					Excellence						Security
					Expertise						Service
					Fairness						Simplicity
					Faith						Solitude
					Fame						Spirituality
					Fitness						Spontaneity
					Freedom						Stability
					Fun						Structure
					Growth						Teamwork
					Harmony						Truth
					Health						Variety
					Inspiration						Other:
					Integrity						Other:
					Intelligence						Other:

2. Review each of the stories you wrote and list the passions and interests that you identified in each experience.

   • My passions and interests are:

3. For each of the experiences you described, use the Core Values Worksheet to identify the core values that were present. Using the Core Values Worksheet, indicate if the experience embodied the value listed.

4. Count the number of values you have identified. List your top five most frequently identified values. If there is a tie in the number identified, reflect on your experiences and select the top five values that best reflect what is important to you.

   1.
   2.
   3.
   4.
   5.

 Now that you have identified your top five core values, refer to the Resiliency Action Plan Summary Worksheet (**Table 6.3**) at the end of this chapter.

ACTIVITY 2: UNDERSTAND THE PASSIONS AND INTERESTS THAT MOTIVATE YOU

This activity uses the wheel to enable you to determine your current level of satisfaction with your passions and interests. You will be able to quickly assess your level of satisfaction with various elements of your life, including those that motivate you. This information will help align your vision and mission with your passions, interests, and values.

INSTRUCTIONS

1. Make a copy of the Balance of Passions and Interests Wheel (**Table 6.2**). Review the labels on the wheel for the various elements in your life. The elements should include required items (such as work, for example) as well as your passions and interests. You may modify any labels that don't fit or create new ones that better reflect the elements in your life. Review the passions and interests you listed in Activity 1.

Table 6.2

Balance of Passions and Interests Wheel

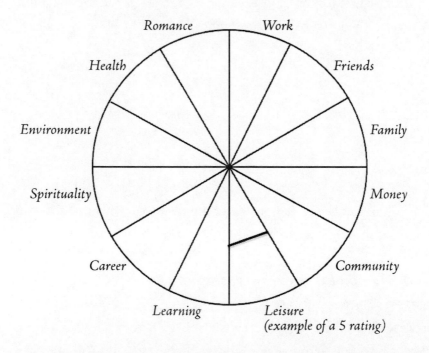

(example of a 5 rating)

2. On a scale of zero to ten (zero is the center of the wheel and ten is the outer edge of the wheel), rate your level of satisfaction with each label. Ten indicates "very satisfied" and zero indicates "very unsatisfied." Draw a line across each element that represents your level of satisfaction. For example, if you are somewhat satisfied with

your leisure time, maybe a "five" best represents this element. Draw a line halfway across this element.

3. After you have evaluated each element, complete the reflection questions and your Resiliency Action Plan. It is important to note that all items on your wheel do not have to be rated a ten, either now or in the future. For example, while you may not be highly satisfied with the amount of money you earn, you earn enough to support yourself and your family comfortably. You rate money a seven, and at this time in your life it is acceptable for money to be rated a seven.

Answer these reflection questions.

1. How satisfied are you with those elements you have identified as passions or interests?

2. What elements of your life seem to need your attention right now?

3. What elements of your life are working well?

4. Identify the top two priority elements you want to focus on to increase your satisfaction. What would it take to be more satisfied with your top two priority elements?

5. Write one SMART goal for each of the two priority elements you identified. The goals should be focused on increasing your satisfaction with the two elements.

 Write your two SMART goals, one for each priority element. Refer to the Resiliency Action Plan Summary Worksheet (**Table 6.3**) at the end of this chapter.

ACTIVITY 3: DEVELOP A CLEAR SENSE OF VISION FOR YOUR LIFE AND CAREER

This activity enables you to create a vision statement that provides a compelling image of your future, five years out. Your vision statement should describe your desired future state, but not the action steps to get there. It is typically a one- or two-sentence statement that aligns with your core values. For example, Susan has a passion for working at a nonprofit that focuses on eradicating cancer. This desire is anchored in her core values of achievement, innovation, service, health, and family. Susan's vision statement is, *I will be a leader in helping cancer researchers discover innovative cures for cancer. I will have loving relationships with my husband and children.*

INSTRUCTIONS

1. Imagine it is five years from now. Write down ideas on what you want your life to be like in five years.
   a. Revisit the values clarification activity. What are your top five values and how do you want to see them integrated into your life in five years?
   b. Revisit the balance of passions and interests life wheel activity. What are your key passions and interests and how are they anchored in your values?

2. Write a draft of your vision statement. Don't stop to overanalyze. Once you have the first draft, then edit and ensure your values and passions are incorporated.

3. Review your vision statement with someone close to you to get feedback. Make edits as appropriate. Finalize your vision statement.

4. You will want to review your vision statement annually. Since your vision statement is future-oriented, you may not need to make changes on an annual basis.

 Write your vision statement referring to the Resiliency Action Plan Summary Worksheet (**Table 6.3**) at the end of this chapter.

ACTIVITY 4: CREATE A MISSION ALIGNED WITH YOUR VALUES, PASSIONS, AND VISION

This activity will assist you in creating a mission that focuses on helping you achieve your vision. A mission statement is typically a paragraph, four to five sentences, and is more focused on the broad activities necessary to achieve the vision. A mission statement helps you to operationalize your vision and focuses on what you want to accomplish in the next year or two. Mission statements address the questions of who, what, where, when, why, and how.

Susan's example mission states: *In my current role (when) I (who) will be a leader in information technology (what) at a cancer research center (where). I will lead an innovative IT team focused on creating new software applications and data mining techniques for cancer researchers (how). Cancer researchers will be able to use the applications and techniques to uncover promising trends with new compounds that may cure cancer (why). My (who) work and home life (what/where) will be balanced (how) in order to spend quality time with my family (when/why).*

INSTRUCTIONS

1. Revisit your vision statement. What do you need to accomplish in the next year or two in order to move closer to achieving your vision? Write down all of your ideas.

2. Review your list of ideas and create a draft mission statement consisting of approximately five sentences that summarize your thoughts. Use the who, what, where, when, why and how structure.

3. Revise the draft as necessary.

4. Review the draft mission statement with someone who knows you well to solicit feedback. Make edits if you receive feedback you want to incorporate.

Create your mission statement and refer to the Resiliency Action Plan Summary Worksheet (**Table 6.3**) at the end of this chapter. You will review and update your mission statement annually to ensure alignment with your values, passions, and vision.

ACTIVITY 5: IMPLEMENT GOALS THAT ENABLE YOU TO ACCOMPLISH YOUR MISSION

This activity will provide you with a format that will assist you in creating the annual goals that will help you achieve your mission statement. Write your goals in a SMART format: S – specific, M – measurable, A – achievable, R – result-focused, and T – time-based. Using a SMART format to create your goals will help to ensure that you have created goals that you can accomplish. You will be able to hold yourself accountable for achieving your goals when they are written in a SMART format.

As an example, one of Susan's goals is, *Create two new job descriptions* (M) *by the second quarter* (T) *for my IT roles* (A) *that include specifics on the skills required to innovatively create new software applications and data mining techniques for cancer researchers* (S) *in order to hire the best talent* (R). The goal is specific, measurable, achievable, result-focused, and time-based.

INSTRUCTIONS

1. Write a draft of five SMART goals that you want to achieve within the next year that will help you to achieve your mission.
2. Review each goal and ensure that each contains the SMART components. Rewrite as necessary.
3. Implement the goals in order to achieve your mission and vision.
4. Update the goals if things change significantly, or add a new goal when one is accomplished.
5. Revise your goals annually.

Create your five SMART goals and refer to your Resiliency Action Plan Summary Worksheet (**Table 6.3**) at the end of this chapter.

RESILIENCY ACTION PLAN SUMMARY WORKSHEET

Refer to the worksheet (**Table 6.3**) to summarize key outcomes and SMART goals from the activities in this chapter.

For each activity associated with this strategy, make sure you have identified a key outcome or SMART goal to help you take action. Capture these commitments in your day planner or calendar to ensure you complete them.

Table 6.3

☑	Resiliency Action Plan Summary Worksheet
Activity	**Key Outcome or SMART Goals**
1	
2	
3	
4	
5	

ADDITIONAL RESOURCES

The following resources may consist of online videos, apps, and assessment tools that could provide greater depth on key concepts associated with this Resiliency Strategy. We have no control over and do not endorse third-party content, goods, or services.

- Coach.me (App). Powerful application that helps you set goals, track them, and get support from other users or professional coaches. Available at https://www.coach.me.

- Goals on Track (App). Useful application for setting goals, tracking them, and measuring your success. Available at http://www.goalsontrack.com.

- Lifetick (App). Powerful app for identifying and tracking progress toward your SMART goals. Available at https://www.lifetick.com.

- Success Wizard (App). Comprehensive application for assessing your life satisfaction, clarifying your mission, vision, and values, and setting specific goals to move forward. Available at http://successwizard.org.

SEVEN

LINDA'S STORY: A JUST IN TIME AWAKENING

BY LINDA FULLMAN

Our deepest fear is not that we are inadequate. Our deepest fear is that we are powerful beyond measure. It is our light, not our darkness that most frightens us.
— MARIANNE WILLIAMSON

I started my career as a naïve college graduate. I believed performing well on the job was all I needed to do to have the meaningful career I desired. I began working in human resources for a chain of hospitals and spent several years in training and development. After three mergers and acquisitions, I changed careers and became a licensed realtor. For the next thirteen years, I focused on real estate sales and the training and development of new realtors.

Then, over a five-year period the focus of my life changed dramatically. I had ended a successful real estate career to focus on my marriage just as I found out it was ending. Soon after, I lost my father. The following year, my brother passed away unexpectedly. My mother soon became very ill, and I became numb. I moved across the country and took a position with a major banking institution to spend time with my mother before she died.

For five years, I didn't live. I barely survived. I no longer knew myself. Nothing I did professionally gave me joy. Sometimes we take positions to further our résumés, learn a new skill, or because we think it's the right thing to do. In this case, I thought taking the banking job was the right thing to do, as it allowed me to be near my mother. I hoped to find something rewarding to energize and anchor me. The work seemed interesting, but was emotionally and intellectually unrewarding. The work environment was divisive and stressful. I felt disconnected in every way.

I realized that each stressful life event had prompted me to change careers. I had reacted to things happening in my life and made choices to overcome perceived obstacles. I changed my career in training and development because I was tired of corporate buyouts and feeling powerless. I then decided to work for myself in real estate. When my work schedule affected my marriage and personal life, I changed careers again to have a more flexible schedule. And when my parents became ill, I changed my career yet again to spend time with them.

While my work at the bank was interesting, I was empty. I was only going through the motions, and nothing felt meaningful or joyful. Experiencing loss of this magnitude, in this short time, made me acutely aware that time is a precious commodity. I had been reacting to others' needs most of my adult life, and I had lost sight of what made me happy and fulfilled. I wasn't sure what to do next to have the life and career I wanted. I felt stuck.

I knew I had to make some significant changes in my life. I wanted something completely different. I meditated and read books to try to find clarity. My new thoughts were competing with my old fears, grief, and other misgivings. I looked to a few close friends and former colleagues for support. My immediate focus was on building my support network to help me clarify my purpose. During a span of about six months, my support network helped me to identify my passions, strengths, and weaknesses. They suggested I write down the things I found meaningful, and what I wanted to accomplish personally and professionally. These people knew me so well that they added their observations to this list. They became my personal board of directors to help me clarify my vision.

This information about my passions, strengths, and weaknesses helped me to identify and articulate my purpose. I had never picked apart my life in this manner. It seemed selfish and even somewhat irresponsible to think of defining a career in terms of how it would fulfill me and make me happy. I started to remember defining moments in my life, good and bad. I remembered the choices I had made. I thought about what I would do differently. Most of all, I realized I didn't want to do what was assumed to be the right thing, or the most comfortable thing. My board of directors, while simultaneously helping me grieve my past, started coaching me to my future. They helped me build self-awareness and realize that if I was going to achieve something different, I needed to do something I had never done before. I needed to connect with my passion and understand that following my passion isn't selfish. It's about self-preservation and fulfillment.

Self-preservation may seem a bit dramatic, but the truth is I felt like I was emotionally dying a little each day. I wasn't taught to identify my emotions or to take care of them. Intellectually I could go through the motions if asked as I'm intelligent and a problem solver. However, when asked what would make me happy, my answer was always something rote. It was a list of things that I either performed or possessed that was considered a recipe for happiness. This list was the summation of a lifetime of influences from others. I had always taken others' happiness and preferences into account, never my own. I realized I needed to make time to take care of myself.

In life, we are presented with many opportunities to reinvent ourselves. Sometimes we have to ignore all the other voices of our past, including our doubts, and allow our most authentic self to emerge. I had been living my life to please others for so long that I had forgotten who I was. Even though I felt a twinge of fear, I packed up and moved to a city where I knew no one. I used my life savings to buy a company in an unfamiliar industry. What my friends and coaches knew is that my skills translated perfectly into this new venture and everything I had done before had prepared me for this moment.

To be truly authentic and not fall into old habits, I had to get away from my comfort zone and be alone with my thoughts. I had to challenge myself emotionally, physically, and spiritually to become the person I wanted to be. I had to learn how to become my best friend. It was in losing myself completely that I finally made myself whole. Finally, I experienced bliss on my terms instead of doing what others expected of me.

Today, I'm building a company that I love. I'm building an environment that fosters constant change. My company supports a variety of causes that fuel my passion. I'm learning to become a good steward of myself: my dreams, my company, my staff, and my community. At forty-four years of age, I am now the proud owner of an insurance company that works to protect our customers and effect change in my community. I moved to a new town and began working in a field related to, but completely outside of, my old comfort zone. I am challenged and inspired every day, becoming more of the person I am meant to be. My experience reminds me of a quote by Maria Rilke: "Live the questions now. Perhaps then, someday far in the future, you will gradually, without even noticing it, live your way into the answer." I think I finally found the answer, and I am living my dream.

I recommend the following actions to anyone who is working on building resiliency and who wants to thrive, not just survive.

- When you're in the middle of your storm, you need a compass to help guide you. Don't be afraid to reach out to your support network for help with clarifying your purpose.

- Spend some quality time alone and engage in self-care activities. It will help you become more self-aware and enable you to identify your needs and wants.

- You determine your happiness. Don't be afraid of disappointing others to make yourself happy.

- Do something you thought you would never do, and don't let fear overtake you. Take a leap of faith and understand that you are worth it. You have the skills it takes to transform yourself, and it's never too late to change.

- Remember to surround yourself with a supportive team to help keep you on track. Change is not easy, and without support, it's easy to resurrect old behaviors.

BIOGRAPHY

Linda Fullman is the owner of Fullman & Lawrence Agency, a full-service insurance company with two locations serving the state of Texas. She provides products to individuals and small businesses to help them protect and accumulate assets. In her spare time, she loves volunteering on several boards, cooking, and traveling. You can reach her at Linda Fullman, c/o Fullman & Lawrence Agency, 901 Gilmer Road, Longview, TX 75604, www.fullmanlawrence.com, or email her at lindahfullman@gmail.com.

EIGHT

RESILIENCY STRATEGY: BUILD SELF-AWARENESS

*Develop an awareness of your thoughts, emotions, and development
needs to improve your capacity to consciously manage your behavior.*

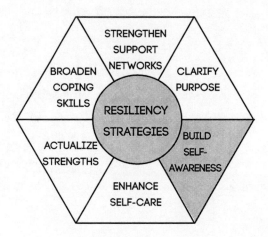

*When someone holds the mirror up, stop to take a look.
Be open to the gift of self-awareness.*
— LYNN SCHMIDT

BUILD SELF-AWARENESS: FRANCESCA'S STORY

When Francesca's company offered her a new job opportunity in a
different country, she was excited. The new job provided her with the
chance to relocate to another country in Europe. It was only a two-hour
flight from the country where she grew up, went to college, and worked for

the last eight years. The job would give her the ability to gain international experience and to live as an expatriate. She would be required to increase her fluency in a foreign language and learn a new culture. Her current country's culture focused on connecting with others, and the quality of relationships was important. The culture in the country she was moving to focused on knowledge and completion of tasks. Francesca felt that this job opportunity would be a good next step for her career, and she accepted the position.

Francesca had built many relationships in her division of the company over the last eight years. The relocation required her to leave all of those relationships behind and create new ones. The job provided her with the opportunity to work in a new area of the company, and knowledge of that department was needed to be successful in the role. Her previous role was as an individual contributor and required a blend of project management and customer relationship skills. Francesca loved the combination of the two skill sets. She felt it made the best use of her strengths. Her new job title was Project Leader, and the role was focused solely on project management. Her job was to indirectly lead other employees to task completion, and these employees didn't report to her directly. In addition, no contact with the customer was necessary. Francesca felt up to the job, and her excitement continued to build as she prepared to make the move.

Francesca arrived at her job site excited and ready for the challenge. Her new manager traveled extensively, so Francesca began her new role with little direction. While she could speak and understand the language, her proficiency wasn't as strong as it needed to be to communicate fluently. This caused her to misinterpret conversations and make mistakes. She continued taking language classes, and her ability to speak and understand the language increased daily. Francesca thought that she was making good progress, and while she was aware of the mistakes, she believed that it was all part of the learning process. Her new team members were less tolerant of her inability to converse fluently. Some of them believed that the project was moving slower than necessary because of Francesca's lack of proficiency in the language. Others thought that she wasn't knowledgeable enough about the department's policies and practices to effectively lead the project. Several felt that she didn't demonstrate strong leadership skills and that she wasn't capable of providing direction to the project team.

Team members began to complain to Francesca about the project, and team meetings were frequently confrontational. Francesca was not used to being confronted directly, and she felt disrespected. She felt overwhelmed, and her automatic response to the conflict was to withdraw. Except for the contact she had to have with team members, she distanced herself from them. She continued to focus on her language skills and learning about the department, and stopped trying to build relationships with the team. Team members viewed her as cold, unapproachable, and not open to hearing their ideas. She had been in the job six months when team members began to complain to their direct managers about her language skills and lack of departmental knowledge. Those managers passed the complaints on to Francesca's manager.

Francesca's manager told her that her language skills needed to improve quickly, and she had to put concerted effort into learning about her new department. Francesca left the meeting with her manager feeling confused. She didn't understand what the issues were or why team members had complained to her manager when her manager agreed that the project was on target. Francesca had never received that type of feedback before, and she was embarrassed. Her automatic response was to retreat further, avoiding her manager and meeting with the team only when it was required. She shifted to email as her primary method of communication, which highlighted any language mistakes she made. She stayed at the office late each day to learn about the department, and on the nights she left on time, she went to language classes. She didn't have the time to make friends in her new city. She was isolated at work and at home, and because her natural tendency was to connect and build relationships, the isolation began to take its toll on her both mentally and physically.

The conflict escalated at team meetings, and team members continued to complain to their managers. One team member requested to be replaced on the project. Francesca's manager talked with her again, and this time emphasized that the team interactions needed to improve or her performance review would be negatively affected. Francesca said little at the meeting with her manager and retreated to her office when it was over. She had no idea how to improve the team interactions and wasn't clear on what to do next. She left the office that day depressed, believing she had made a mistake in taking a job in another country. If she wasn't successful in this job, she knew it would be hard to find another position.

DERAILMENT TRIGGERS

Cultural differences can be encountered daily without moving to another country. These derailment triggers can be caused by a lack of self-awareness and are important whether you relocate to another country, start working in a different industry, or work for a manager with a different background. Expatriate assignments do present a unique opportunity for individuals to learn and grow. Living and working in another country develops knowledge and skills that can't be acquired any other way.

Expatriate assignments can be very challenging and present a number of derailment triggers if the relocating employee and organization are not prepared for the effect of the change. Even though Francesca acknowledged that language proficiency and cultural differences would exist, she believed that she could handle any challenges that would occur. She thought that taking language classes and spending extra time learning about the department would offset any issues. Had Francesca taken the time to think through the challenges and become more self-aware about how her thoughts, emotions, and development needs affected her behavior, she would have identified the following potential derailment triggers:

1. **A job working in a different culture.**
   Francesca's new job was in a country with a culture different from the one she had experienced her entire life. In the country she was from, it was important to build relationships over time. Who you knew and how long you had known them mattered. Confrontation was often avoided. In her new country, what you knew mattered. Subject matter experts were the people who succeeded. Confrontation was not only common, but admired. Francesca's natural response to this cultural difference concerning conflict was to withdraw. She wasn't aware of how she responded to conflict or how important it was that she was perceived as the subject matter expert.

2. **Conscious and unconscious development needs.**
   Even though Francesca had foundational knowledge of the language spoken in her new country when she moved there, her proficiency wasn't strong enough to fully understand everything team members said or wrote. While this development need didn't affect the project timeline immediately, mistakes in interpretation were made that frustrated her team members. Francesca felt that her mistakes were part of the learning process, and she wasn't aware of the impact that her lack of proficiency was having on others. She was not aware of her response to conflict and the impact it had on others. By taking the time to identify her development needs and proactively address them, she could develop the skills required for success in the new position.

3. **A new manager with a different cultural background.**
   Francesca started working for a manager she didn't know, and her new manager was from a different country. Francesca and her new manager didn't take the time to proactively discuss the issues that might arise as part of an expatriate assignment and put contingency

plans in place to circumvent problems. Because Francesca wasn't aware that her behavior was causing issues with the team, she was unable to solicit support from her manager. When team members began complaining, her manager was less aware of the real issues and focused on the language proficiency and departmental knowledge. When conflict arose, Francesca began avoiding her manager and was unaware how that would affect their relationship.

4. **An assignment leading new team members.**
    Francesca's new role was similar to the project leadership roles she had in the past, leading team members that were not direct reports. Except now she was leading team members with different cultural and behavioral expectations. Francesca led these team members in the same way she had led project teams in her previous job. She didn't take the time to understand their differing expectations of her as a leader or the cultural differences. Team members did not perceive her as a strong leader. When confronted, she withdrew, causing the team members to view her as cold and unapproachable. Francesca was unaware of the team's perceptions and the impact of her behavioral response to conflict.

There is often more than one trigger present in derailment scenarios. That is what makes it hard for the individual affected to separate and identify all of the issues. It can feel like being caught up in a hurricane, whipped one direction and then another. It's hard for anyone in this scenario to step back and think about the situation objectively. It is important to become more aware of the impact of thoughts and emotions on behaviors before the derailment situation occurs. That is why it's critical to take time beforehand to evaluate the resiliency strategies and create a Resiliency Action Plan. Below are sample questions based on Francesca's story that can be used to build self-awareness for each of the four derailment triggers.

DERAILMENT TRIGGER QUESTIONS

These questions will help you to better understand your development needs and navigate potential derailment. Ask yourself these questions before you move into a new position.

- What is different about the culture where I will be working, as compared to where I currently work and live?

- How do I need to change my behavior to align better with the culture, and am I willing to make those changes?

- What development needs do I need to focus on based on the new assignment, and how am I going to close the developmental gaps?

- In what ways are my new manager and I different, and in what ways are we similar?

- What steps do I need to take to understand my new manager's and team members' expectations?

DEFINING 'BUILD SELF-AWARENESS'

Building self-awareness helps you to develop an understanding of your thoughts, emotions, and development needs to improve your capacity to consciously manage your behavior. First, in order to maintain your resiliency, it is important to have enough self-awareness to be able to detect when you lose it and take actions to regain balance. Second, you have to be aware of your development needs before you can improve them. Increased self-awareness provides you with the opportunity to make conscious choices about your behavior, determine how to build skills to increase your competence, and create a successful and satisfying career. Based on a model created by Noel Burch, there are four sequential phases of competence.

1. Unconscious Incompetence—you don't know you are incompetent, and you must recognize your development needs before you can progress. Self-awareness requires being open to feedback from others so that blind spots can be identified and eliminated.

2. Conscious Incompetence—you have identified the development need, its importance, and you make a conscious decision on whether to improve or not. Mistakes will be made as you learn the new skill or behavior.

3. Conscious Competence—you have learned how to do the skill or behavior, but it takes a high degree of concentration to do it correctly.

4. Unconscious Competence—you are now so good at the skill or behavior that you do it without even thinking about how you do it.

As you increase your self-awareness and work on your development needs, you will find yourself moving through these phases. Ongoing feedback will help you to stay on track and make the improvements you desire.

BUILD SELF-AWARENESS ACTION STEPS

There are five action steps within *Build Self-Awareness* that can be taken to help you develop an understanding of your thoughts, emotions, and development needs to improve your capacity to consciously manage your behavior:

1. Solicit feedback from others about your strengths and development areas and create development goals.

2. Realize how your thoughts influence your emotions and behaviors.

3. Understand your emotional hot buttons.

4. Make conscious choices about your reactions to others.

5. Monitor your level of resiliency and take actions to increase resiliency.

You should use the Resiliency Action Plan to create development goals to increase your self-awareness. By identifying your development needs, creating a Resiliency Action Plan, and making conscious choices about your reactions to others, you can successfully manage your career before, during, and after job changes. Resiliency strategies also help you to learn, grow, and thrive when significant challenges are occurring. Billy Jean King's story is an example of how self-awareness enabled her to become a tennis champion, overcome major career challenges, and lead by example as a gender-equality advocate.

Billy Jean King has been quoted as saying, "I think self-awareness is probably the most important thing towards being a champion." Billy Jean was shorter and heavier than a typical tennis player. She was told early in her career that she would never make it, that she might as well give up. She went on to win her first Wimbledon at age seventeen and to become the world number-one professional tennis player. Throughout her career, she focused on being self-aware about her weaknesses and stated, "Champions play their weaknesses better." At age fifty-one she openly acknowledged being a lesbian, and she was the first woman athlete to do so. Because of her admission, she lost all of her endorsements and had to rebuild her reputation and career. When asked in a 2013 interview by *Rookie* Magazine what it felt like to win, she responded, "I just kept thinking about how I needed to keep developing my game so that I could be number one in the world. [Victory] is fleeting—the process of getting there is what propels you. What makes it exciting is the daily routine, because when you do win, you know it's because you did the work [to get there], and when you don't win, you learn to bounce back. You are always starting over."

Billy Jean King focused on having a clear understanding of what she needed to do to improve, developing her weaknesses and using them to her advantage. Even when individuals make the effort to be proactive and become more self-aware, they can still face unexpected career challenges that may require them to start over. If that occurs, it's important to have the capability to revisit the skills and activities that increase self-awareness and continue to improve in new development areas that arise due to changing circumstances.

BUILD SELF-AWARENESS:
FRANCESCA'S RESILIENCY ACTION PLAN

After two discussions with her manager, Francesca was aware that the project team was having problems. She was not clear on what was causing the problems or how to improve the team interactions. She did not understand how she was unconsciously reacting to the conflict and how the team members were interpreting her behavior. But she was concerned and knew that something had to be done. Francesca intuitively reached out to a previous mentor that she had a trusting relationship with and described what was taking place. Her mentor was able to ask questions similar to the derailment trigger questions, to help move Francesca's awareness about her behaviors from unconscious to conscious. Support from a mentor and increased awareness of the impact of her behavior enabled Francesca to create an action plan to increase her resiliency as she worked through her career challenges. Francesca's plan focused on building self-awareness, including these actions:

- Soliciting feedback about her strengths and development needs from her manager, a peer, and a team member in order to have a better understanding of how her behavior was perceived and how it was impacting others.

- Discussing the outcomes of the feedback with her mentor to understand her behavioral responses and make conscious decisions on how to move forward.

- Identifying her hot buttons, the triggers that caused her to behave in ways that the team members considered negative.

- Creating a development plan that outlined what behaviors and skills she needed to improve upon and how she was going to make the improvements.

- Monitoring her level of resiliency on a regular schedule to explore the triggers that caused her to feel more or less resilient.

- Scheduling time to meet with her mentor regularly to review her action plan and progress and involve her manager in her action planning progress.

Francesca began working on her action plan. She had one-on-one discussions with her manager, a peer, and a team member that she trusted, and she gathered feedback about how she was perceived. She shared the feedback with her mentor, and her mentor was able to ask questions to help her see how her response to conflict was affecting the team. Through ongoing discussions with her mentor, Francesca was able to understand how conflict triggered her emotions and caused her to respond in ways that were perceived negatively. She put together an action plan with specific completion dates to help change her behavioral responses to the conflict, and she focused on building relationships with her manager and team members. She continued to work on increasing her language proficiency and knowledge of the department. She shared her action plan with her manager, peer, and the team member who gave her feedback to gain support. She asked them to provide her with ongoing feedback on what was working well and what she needed to do differently. She implemented a process to monitor her level of resiliency and tracked what triggered her to feel more or less resilient each day. She put actions in place to maximize the triggers that made her feel more resilient and minimize the triggers that made her feel less resilient.

Several months after Francesca began working on her action plan, she was able to meet with team members and talk with them one-on-one about how the team was working and solicit suggestions for how she could improve her interactions with the team. Francesca had a positive meeting with her manager, who provided her with encouragement and support. The team interactions continued to improve, as did Francesca's response to conflict. Her fluency in the language reached a point where mistakes were no longer occurring that affected the project, and she knew what questions to ask to be sure she was following departmental policies. Because of her focus on her Resiliency Action Plan, Francesca was able to turn around a potentially career-derailing situation.

When you build self-awareness, you can make conscious decisions about how to improve your competence and change behaviors for career success. Francesca put her Resiliency Action Plan in place after the potentially career-derailing experience happened, and she was able to grow and thrive despite the negative experience. She could have implemented the action plan prior to moving into the new role to help her effectively manage career challenges. This would have increased her resiliency and her ability to thrive, not just survive.

BUILD SELF-AWARENESS: RESILIENCY ACTION PLAN ACTIVITIES

The purpose of this strategy is to help you develop an understanding of your thoughts, emotions, and development needs to improve your capacity to consciously manage your behavior. There are five actions that you can take to help clarify your purpose.

1. Solicit feedback from others about your strengths and development areas, and create development goals.

2. Realize how your thoughts influence your emotions and behaviors.

3. Understand your emotional hot buttons.

4. Make conscious choices about your reactions to others.

5. Monitor your level of resiliency and take actions to increase resiliency.

The following five activities will help you take action to build self-awareness.

ACTIVITY 1: SOLICIT FEEDBACK FROM OTHERS ABOUT YOUR STRENGTHS AND DEVELOPMENT AREAS, AND CREATE DEVELOPMENT GOALS

The purpose of this activity is to gather feedback from others to help you identify your strengths and development areas and create development goals for your Resiliency Action Plan. This activity provides you with a simple structure to collect feedback that you can implement on your own, in a minimal amount of time. It is important to gather feedback from others in order to become more self-aware.

INSTRUCTIONS

1. Identify three people to give you feedback on your strengths and development needs. You are looking for individuals that you trust to give you honest feedback. One recommendation is your manager, a peer, and someone you manage either directly or indirectly.

2. Reach out to the people you have identified and explain that you would like to talk with them one-on-one for thirty minutes to get feedback to create a development plan focused on your continuous improvement. Schedule the meetings.

3. Let the three people know that you will be asking them these three questions, so they have time to prepare in advance of the meeting.

You'll ask them:

    a.   What are my top two strengths? Please provide specific examples.

    b.   What are my top two development needs? Please provide specific examples.

    c.   What else would you like to share with me that will help with my development?

4.   Your job during the meeting is to listen and take notes, not to become defensive. Thank them for their time and let them know you will be scheduling another thirty-minute meeting to share the results of your development plan.

5.   When you have all three interviews complete, look for common themes in the strengths and development needs. Identify ways you can further utilize your strengths to offset your development needs. Determine two development needs that are most critical to focus on based on your career goals. Create one SMART development goal for each of the development needs. If you have a mentor or a close friend that you can share your development plan with and get input, that can be helpful.

6.   Meet with the three people individually, share your development plan, and ask them to provide ongoing feedback on what they see is working well and what needs improvement. Set up quarterly meetings to get the ongoing feedback.

 Create your two SMART development goals and refer to the Resiliency Action Plan Summary Worksheet (**Table 8.1**) at the end of this chapter.

ACTIVITY 2: REALIZE HOW YOUR THOUGHTS INFLUENCE YOUR EMOTIONS AND BEHAVIORS

This activity will assist you with reflecting on past experiences, future events, and emotional triggers. Journaling is considered one of the best activities to help you reflect on what has happened, what you want to happen, and what changes you need to make. It can bring clarity to how your thoughts are influencing your emotional responses and behaviors. It can help you to understand the progress you are making on your development goals and what changes you need to make. Journaling is a personal activity that everyone does a little differently. You will need to select your preferred way to journal.

INSTRUCTIONS

1. Get ready to write in your journal by asking yourself the following questions:

    a. Why do I want to keep a journal? What is the purpose, and what would I like to achieve by journaling?

    b. When do I want to write in my journal? What works best for me: mornings, evenings, midday? Do I want to write in my journal every day?

    c. What do I want to write about in my journal? Will my journal be focused on my development goals and other activities?

    d. Where do I want to write in my journal? Do I want to write in my journal at home, in a coffee shop, outdoors, in bed?

    e. Who do I want to include in my journal? Will I be writing about my professional life or my personal life or both?

    f. How do I want to write in my journal? Do I want to buy a nice journal and write by hand, or do I want to type my journal on my phone or computer?

2. Once you answer these questions, you are ready to begin journaling. The purpose is to reflect on your experiences to become more self-aware. You can create personalized questions to reflect on for your

journaling. In order to create your personalized questions, ask yourself, "What questions would I want my coach, mentor, or friend to ask me?" To help you get started, consider using some of the following questions to prompt reflection and insight.

   a. What am I grateful for today?

   b. What would I do in my life or work if I felt no fear?

   c. What do I want to feel when I look back at my life when I am 80 years old?

   d. Who am I jealous of and why?

   e. What regrets do I have about my life or work?

   f. How does my adult life reflect the games and toys I used to play with as a child?

   g. If I didn't have to worry about money, what would I do with my time?

   h. What are five excuses I hear myself making for not having what I really want in my life or work?

   i. Who are some powerful role models for the kind of work or life I want to create?

   j. What are ten things I feel gratitude for and why?

   k. What are the five most painful experiences I've had in my life, and how did I grow from them?

3. Regularly go back and reread what you wrote in your journal to see how you would do things differently now that you have had time to reflect. What is working well and what do you want to do differently?

Create one SMART goal that you want to achieve to enhance your journaling practice. Refer to your Resiliency Action Plan Summary Worksheet (**Table 8.1**) at the end of this chapter.

ACTIVITY 3: UNDERSTAND YOUR EMOTIONAL HOT BUTTONS

This activity enables you to check in with yourself on how you are managing your emotional hot buttons, those things that trigger you to behave in a way that does not align with your development plan. It also helps you understand why you are reacting the way you are and how you can change your behavior.

INSTRUCTIONS

1. Reflect on a past experience where you had a very strong reaction to another person or situation.

2. For this experience, identify which hot buttons you thought were present at the time.

3. Reflect on the following:
   a. What did you observe in the other person that suggested the presence of the hot-button action?
   b. What were your thoughts?
   c. What were your emotions?
   d. How did you react?

4. What would have been a better way to react to that person or situation?

5. Write down your responses to those questions and identify your top two hot buttons. Write a SMART goal for each of your top two hot buttons, focused on how you will effectively manage them.

6. Review the goals periodically to adjust your responses to your hot buttons. Repeat this activity when your hot buttons have been triggered.

 Create your two SMART goals and refer to your Resiliency Action Plan (**Table 8.1**) at the end of this chapter.

ACTIVITY 4: MAKE CONSCIOUS CHOICES ABOUT YOUR REACTIONS TO OTHERS

The definition of mindfulness that is used here is the intentional, accepting, and nonjudgmental focus of one's attention on the emotions, thoughts, and sensations occurring in the present. The purpose of this activity is to assist you with practicing informal mindfulness activities that will help you to be intentional about how you react to others. Practicing mindfulness can help you manage your emotional triggers by becoming aware of them. You reflect on what is happening in the present versus the past or the future.

INSTRUCTIONS

1. You can do this mindfulness activity in two-, five-, or ten-minute increments. Set a timer, so you don't have to worry about the clock. You don't have to spend a great deal of time to reap the benefits. It can be done at the office, in your car, at home, or anywhere you can take private time to sit, close your eyes, and breathe deeply. Schedule time to do this daily. It is a good activity to do at the moment you feel stress so that you can manage your reaction.

2. Sit down with your feet flat on the floor. Sit up straight and close your eyes. You can also do this activity standing up.

3. Begin to breathe deeply.

4. Think about the top of your head, your shoulders, tips of your fingers, posterior in the chair, your knees, your feet, and your toes.

5. Then reflect on what you are feeling in the moment. What emotions are present now? Are they the emotions you want to be present? How do you want to react?

6. Reflect on how you want to feel right now, on your thoughts and emotions.

7. When the time you have allotted is over, decide what conscious choice you will make about how you will react to the current situation. Jot it down on a piece of notepaper or in your journal.

8. Reflect on what you have written periodically. Ask yourself if you are making conscious choices about how you will react to others and if you are taking the appropriate action to implement those choices.

 Create one SMART goal to enhance your mindfulness practice. Refer to your Resiliency Action Plan Summary Worksheet (**Table 8.1**) at the end of this chapter.

ACTIVITY 5: MONITOR YOUR LEVEL OF RESILIENCY
AND TAKE ACTIONS TO BUILD RESILIENCY

This activity will help you develop a customized personal indicator to track your daily progress and identify barriers to your growth toward greater resiliency. You will use the resiliency indicator to monitor and track what triggers make you feel more or less resilient each day. You may think you are feeling very resilient, but asking yourself the question regularly will help you become more aware of your resiliency highs and lows. You will then be able to put actions in place to maximize the triggers that made you feel more resilient and minimize the triggers that made you feel less resilient.

INSTRUCTIONS

1. Create your resiliency scale indicator by identifying how you will know what it looks like to function at a "one" (not resilient at all) or a "ten" (highly resilient). What will you think or feel when you're at either end of the continuum? How will you behave? What will people say to you?

2. If you are journaling, decide whether you want to include this activity in your journal or track it separately.

3. Set up calendar reminders to ask yourself once or twice a day how resilient you are feeling at the time you get the reminder, on a scale of one to ten. You might decide to ask the question in the morning, again at lunch, and then at the end of the evening. Or maybe you will decide to ask the question at the end of each day.

4. Write down the number you selected in your journal if you are journaling. If not, take notes in an electronic document or a different notebook. Make notes about why you selected that number. What thoughts did you have that caused your resiliency indicator number to be high or low? How did your thoughts or emotional reactions affect your resiliency?

5. Take time each day to reflect on your resiliency indicator and explore why it is high or low. Make notes about what makes you feel more resilient and what makes you feel less resilient. Act on what you want to do differently to increase your resiliency indicator. Repeat those activities that give you a high resiliency indicator.

 Create one SMART goal to increase your resiliency indicator score. Refer to your Resiliency Action Plan Summary Worksheet (**Table 8.1**) at the end of this chapter.

RESILIENCY ACTION PLAN SUMMARY WORKSHEET

Refer to the worksheet below to summarize key outcomes and SMART goals from the activities in this chapter.

For each activity associated with this strategy, make sure you have identified a key outcome or SMART goal to help you take action. Capture these commitments in your day planner or calendar to ensure you complete them.

Table 8.1

☑	Resiliency Action Plan Summary Worksheet	
Activity	**Key Outcome or SMART Goals**	
1		
2		
3		
4		
5		

ADDITIONAL RESOURCES

The following resources may consist of online videos, apps, and assessment tools that could provide greater depth on key concepts associated with this Resiliency Strategy. We have no control over and do not endorse third-party content, goods, or services.

- Conflict Dynamic Profile (Online Assessment). Free online assessment to help you identify your hot buttons during conflict situations. Available at http://www.conflictdynamics.org/products/cdp/hb/index.php.

- Headspace (App). Meditation and mindfulness app to help you increase awareness of your thoughts and emotions. Available at https://www.headspace.com.

- How to Increase Your Self-Awareness (Online Video, 2 minutes). Useful video to explore how thoughts and feelings produce behavior. Available at https://youtu.be/Vnc6gTq9FTA.

NINE

MARIANNE'S STORY: LEGAL DIRECTOR OR ROCK SINGER

BY MARIANNE RAUTURIER

I have not ceased being fearful, but I have ceased to let fear control me. I have accepted fear as a part of life, specifically the fear of change, the fear of the unknown; and I have gone ahead despite the pounding in the heart that says, "turn back, turn back, you'll die if you venture too far."
— ERICA JONG

Choosing a career can be difficult. How can we know at a young age what we want to do for the rest of our lives and be certain that we won't change our minds? At an early age I knew my parents wanted me to become a doctor. However, as I aged a different profession interested me. I wanted to become a lawyer. My teenage rebellion gave me the strength to persuade my parents that becoming a lawyer was a better career choice. Becoming a lawyer wasn't a wild idea, but acceptable to my parents and a victory for me.

At this time, I developed a strong interest in rock music. My fantasy was to be a rock singer, but it wasn't a realistic career choice. So I continued the acceptable path of becoming a lawyer. After graduation, I began working as a business lawyer in a large legal firm. After a few years, I accepted a position as a corporate lawyer so I could influence the day-to-day operations of the business. For many years, I enjoyed my job and moved up the ranks. At age forty-five, in the middle of my professional career, I experienced a career-derailing event that turned my life upside down.

I was the legal director for a large company, responsible for forty lawyers and paralegals. A new CEO joined the company, and he named a new executive committee consisting exclusively of men. As top managers in the organization resigned, former male colleagues of the new executive team members took their place and the work environment changed for the worse. I held on to my job, naïvely convinced that I had a role to play in the new organization based on excellent annual reviews and positive feedback from my colleagues.

I survived in my job for almost two years in an environment that was no longer supportive. During that period, I felt like I was clinging to a cliff ledge over a vast emptiness while someone was stepping on my fingers, wanting me to let go. My fear was that if I let go, I was going to have a long fall to the ground, concluding with a crash landing. I was the highest income earner in my household and was used to a certain lifestyle. I had two teenagers who were on the path to college. I was a woman who had just turned forty-five. I believed my high income and age represented two major disabilities on the job market. I expected that my fall would be long, painful, and fatal.

Halfheartedly, I tried to find another position. There were not many vacant positions as a legal director specialized in my industry. My interview attempts were pathetic, given my misery in my current role and desperation to find any job. Clearly, I was not a promising candidate for a headhunter or new employer. In retrospect, all these fears turned out wrong, and in fact I was not hanging from a cliff. Surprisingly, my feet were a few inches from the ground, and I didn't fall very far when I finally let go. When I landed, there were new lands to explore containing new career options. Once I finally made the decision to let go, it took me very little time to see that it was the right decision. Within two weeks, I met with friends and former colleagues who had made significant changes in their careers and I listened to their stories. I talked to a coach who helped me accept that my time with my current company was over. Ultimately, with the help of a lawyer, I negotiated an acceptable resignation, including a severance package and access to career transition services.

The career transition consultant helped me learn and apply resiliency strategies, such as clarifying my goals, building self-awareness, and most importantly for me, networking. I learned new methods to adapt, grow, and thrive on a continuous basis. Through this process, I realized I needed to clarify my purpose. When asked about my goals, I would say I was thinking about becoming a rock singer. I did not seriously think that would be possible. For me, suggesting this option meant I was ready to envision bold new career options free of my traditional path.

The first step I undertook with my career consultant was to revisit my career history, including my accomplishments and my failures. I explored what I enjoyed doing and what I disliked. I also revisited personal achievements, the ones I thought were not worth mentioning, but that illustrated who I am and how I work. It helped me understand my values and the kind of working environment that was most favorable for me. Knowing more about who I am and what I had achieved strengthened my self-confidence and was of great help when I had to present myself. Having determined my ideal working environment, I decided to stay flexible and not set precise long-term goals, since interests, economic conditions, and working habits change. Because the world is constantly evolving, I wanted to be able to seize new opportunities when they came and let go of outdated convictions and positions.

Another resiliency strategy I focused on was strengthening my support networks. Going to the workshops organized by the career office, right after my resignation, allowed me to become open to the world again. I met new people with different positions, from other industries and economic sectors. I broadened my views by listening to people's stories and challenges, as well as sharing my story. During these workshops,

I learned that networking was key to finding a new position. I learned about self-marketing and elevator pitches. When I practiced my newly learned networking strategies, they worked. People I had never met before listened to my suggestions and gave me insights. I was thrilled to rediscover that humans can be kind, nourished by these new connections, and pleased by the exchange of views. I acquired more knowledge about my professional environment, which was a good resource as I looked for a new position. I realized that making human connections and exchanging experiences is critical to balancing my personal and professional life.

When I entered this career transition period, I realized that I needed to focus on self-care, as I had gradually put on weight for the last ten years. Having more time for myself, I went to see a nutritionist. As I got my diet balanced, I decided to hire a personal trainer. The more I exercised, the better I looked and felt. Exercise and running became a part of my life. Beyond exercise, I focused on my passion for music.

During my career transition, I also focused on becoming more self-aware. While attending different workshops, such as nonverbal communication, I learned how others perceived me. I learned the meaning of wordless signals and how to be clear when communicating a message. The list below includes several other developmental activities I took part in.

- Voice-training lessons with an opera singer.

- Reading self-help and personal development books, articles, and blogs.

- Attending various conferences sponsored by professional organizations, many of which were free or inexpensive.

- Incorporating mindfulness and meditation into my life.

Mindfulness and meditation helped me develop a better awareness of my emotions and behaviors. While I have not reached the wisdom of a Buddhist monk yet, I am quieter and less judgmental.

I knew I wanted a change when I left my position. I discovered that I enjoy discovering new things, being innovative, meeting people, and learning constantly. I now like being on the edge of my comfort zone. However, changing jobs or career direction is difficult in France, as it is elsewhere. So I decided to circumvent the difficulty. I now do the same job in the same industry, but I do it differently. I work as an interim legal manager, shifting between companies doing different assignments and projects. I do not mind not having a title that represents status. I found a way to have a meaningful job and to do it in alignment with who I am, my values and motivations. I have learned how to address the concerns of friends and colleagues regarding how I cope with unstable income and fewer financial resources, and how the job market becomes tougher after forty-five. Their questions are reflections of their fears, not mine.

I use the self-marketing techniques I learned during my outplacement experience to find assignments. Being interested in new technologies, I created a website to present my services as an interim manager. I learned about creating websites, blogging for professional purposes, and natural referencing. In-between jobs, I network and go to conferences that enable me to meet new people and listen to their experiences. I read a lot and listen to all kinds of music. All these activities contribute to building who I am now as a human being. I can now fully be the optimistic and curious person I always was deep inside.

Despite not becoming a rock singer, I still sing in my car and in the shower. I intentionally use music as an energy and joy booster. Being an interim manager is like being a singer on tour since I change places constantly, interact with impatient people waiting for me to arrive, and wear a different costume for each project.

As Confucius once said, "We have two lives, and the second begins when we realize we only have one." Recently I have begun to mentor women in search of a professional transition, enabling me to share my experiences and optimistic views. Here is some of the advice I give these women about resiliency.

- Adopt a winning and conquering attitude. It has been proven that body posture influences mindset; therefore make sure your body demonstrates your winning attitude.

- Dare to take risks. Don't let your fears get in the way of making changes to your career.

- Do not live a life where work is a chore and you are deferring self-care until you retire. Who knows how healthy you will be when you reach retirement age? Take retirement time now.

- Balance the time you spend at work with self-care activities, such as exercise, spiritual practices, family time, and creative activities.

- Develop and maintain a network of positive relationships. Take pleasure in meeting people and supporting them. Reach out for help and support when in need.

Biography

Marianne Rauturier is a legal interim manager in France. In her spare time, she sings, listens to music, runs, and spends time with her family and friends. She is now involved in mentoring young people and women in search of a job or a new career. Contact information and more can be found at LinkedIn at https://fr.linkedin.com/in/marianne-desson-rauturier-546a449.

TEN

RESILIENCY STRATEGY: ENHANCE SELF-CARE

Improve your physical, emotional, and spiritual well-being to increase your energy and inoculate yourself against stress.

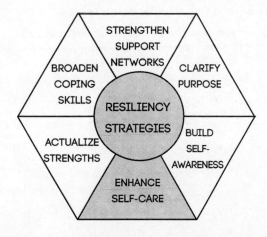

Building resiliency is all about getting uncomfortable. You'll grow and become stronger by accomplishing goals outside of your comfort zone. The payoff is worth it. You'll feel invincible.
— LYNN SCHMIDT

ENHANCE SELF-CARE: ELAINA'S STORY

Elaina intended to be the next Chief Executive Officer (CEO) of her company. Since graduating from college, she had planned every step of her career to move her into a CEO role. She took jobs that provided her with the skills and knowledge needed to run a large organization. She focused all her energy on working long hours to achieve better results than her peers. Elaina's career moved forward as she envisioned. Her most recent promotion was into the role of the Chief Financial Officer (CFO) for her company. With that promotion, she became a member of the executive leadership team reporting directly to the CEO, and her peers were now all the senior leaders of the various functions in the company. Elaina had led many projects for the CEO in the past and felt comfortable with their working relationship. Elaina's career spanned twenty-five years, and it had been a long journey, but she knew that as the CFO she was well positioned to become the next CEO.

Elaina had always been focused on her career, working long hours with little extra time to be involved in activities not related to her job. Her husband worked from home and was the primary caretaker for their children. Her children were now in their last years of high school and independent. Her husband continued to work from home and provide support for the children. In her new role as CFO Elaina worked even longer hours than she had before, often not getting home before eight in the evening. When she did get home, she went to her office to respond to emails and review reports. During the weekends, Elaina spent a majority of her time working as well, learning all the aspects of her new role. She realized that she had many things to learn about being a CFO and being responsible for all the financial aspects of the company. She believed that she needed to know everything about her job and her direct reports' jobs. She took ownership of tasks that had previously been delegated to her direct reports to have more control over results. Her micromanaging approach caused her to work even longer hours.

Many members of the senior executive team, her peers, were new to the organization. Recently, several of the CEO's direct reports had left, and the roles were filled with external candidates. The organization was undergoing a great deal of change, and there was pressure to improve its financial performance. Financial targets were not being met, and the CEO expected Elaina to establish new budgeting procedures that would better align the tracking and reporting of expenditures and revenue. She needed to implement an annual budgeting process that would provide leaders with the responsibility and accountability for their operating expenses. Elaina's peers, who were new to the organization, wanted to spend more time with her to better understand the financial aspects of the company. These two factors added to the stress that Elaina was feeling about her new job. She was worried that she wouldn't be able to deliver what the CEO and her peers expected of her.

Elaina believed that the executive team was not working well together. They did not operate as a team, and each executive focused on his or her functional area. Her peers did not support each other, and there was a lot of competition. When she mentioned it to the CEO, her comments were ignored, and the competition continued to get worse. Arguments frequently took place between her peers during staff meetings, and Elaina tried to avoid getting involved in the negative conversations and taking sides. One of Elaina's peers decided that Elaina and her team were to blame for the organization's financial problems. Her peer sabotaged her with her other peers by making negative comments about her lack of experience and poor performance. Elaina realized that these negative comments were being shared with her manager, the CEO, and she didn't know what to do about it. She saw a change in attitude among her other peers, who started to avoid talking with her. Since her comments to the CEO had been ignored earlier, she didn't want to raise another issue, and her stress level increased.

Elaina had never focused on her health. Due to the number of hours she worked, she did not have a formal exercise plan, though she tried to walk several miles on the weekend. Her diet consisted of fast food that wouldn't take long to make and could be eaten in a hurry. With the additional stress of the new job, the company's financial situation, and the difficult relationships developing with her peers, Elaina's eating habits became worse. She'd grab a bag of chips from the vending machine and stop at a fast food drive-through on the way home. She worked longer hours on the weekends and stopped walking for exercise. She gained weight, and in a matter of months had put on an additional twenty pounds. As the company's financial situation and her relationship with her peers got progressively worse, she started having trouble sleeping, only getting three to four hours of sleep a night. She became irritable and often lost her temper with her husband and children. At work, she felt like she was operating in a fog, not remembering important details. One evening as she was talking with her husband she suddenly felt nauseous and dizzy and was unable to continue the conversation.

Elaina was very concerned about her health issues, which included an inability to sleep, feeling ill, and weight gain. She believed the stress at work contributed to these symptoms and caused her to make mistakes that impacted her performance. She and her husband talked at length about the issues at work and how Elaina's health had deteriorated. The talk with her husband alerted Elaina to the seriousness of the situation, and she scheduled an appointment with her doctor.

DERAILMENT TRIGGERS

Moving into a new role with additional responsibilities when a company needs to turn around its financial performance can surface many derailment triggers. These derailment triggers are often caused by a lack of knowledge, a need to quickly acquire new skills, a desire to have a high level of control over tasks, unexpected organizational financial problems, and increased difficulties with peer relationships. Stress is frequently a result of derailment triggers that have not been proactively addressed. If you are not taking care of your physical, emotional, and spiritual well-being, stress levels can rise, leading to serious health issues, increased work challenges, and possibly derailment.

Elaina had received a significant promotion that moved her into one of the most senior positions in the company. While she was as prepared as she could be, she did not have all of the required knowledge and skills to do the job since she had never been in that job before. She needed to learn quickly to help the organization improve its financial performance. Her need to control all aspects of her organization increased and caused her to become a micromanager. She took on tasks that were the responsibility of her direct reports. The competition between her peers and the sabotage she was experiencing by a peer increased her stress. All these factors contributed to her health issues.

Had Elaina proactively managed her physical, emotional, and spiritual well-being, she would have been better able to manage the challenges that she experienced. She would have thought through the challenges that might occur and identified the following potential derailment triggers:

1. **A significant job promotion.**

   Elaina had a large percentage of the skills and knowledge required to fill the CFO role. She still needed to gain additional skills and knowledge, as she had never done the job before. While Elaina was able to learn and apply new knowledge and skills quickly, this was a significant promotion that moved her into the most senior leadership level in the company. Elaina was not prepared for the additional work pressures that came with this type of job. The company was experiencing financial difficulties that required Elaina to play a visible role in turning around the company's financial performance. This turnaround role was very different from her previous roles, where she had to either maintain the status quo of a function or start up a new function. The senior leadership role and the company's financial problems caused more stress for Elaina than she had expected.

2. **A micromanaging leadership style.**

   Elaina felt significant pressure to perform in her new role and turn around the financial performance of the company. Due to her increased level of stress and need for control, she micromanaged her direct reports, taking on some of their job responsibilities. Micromanaging increased her workload and caused her to work additional hours, late into the evenings and on weekends. Her eating habits were affected by the long work hours and her need to be involved in all aspects of her organization. She would get food from the vending machine and eat it quickly while working. She would leave her desk to go to meetings and then immediately return to her office, not taking any breaks to eat, take a walk, or engage in social activities. With her increased workload on the weekends, she stopped walking for exercise. Within a few months, Elaina had gained twenty pounds.

3. **A new team of peers.**
   With Elaina's promotion came a new team of peers, several of them recently hired from outside of the organization. Elaina had worked with some of her new peers in the past, in support roles, but never in a peer relationship. Most of her peers had more years of experience in a senior leadership role reporting to a CEO. The CEO's new team of direct reports had not formed as a team and did not get along. They operated as separate individuals versus as a team and competed instead of collaborating. This competition led to arguments during staff meetings that caused Elaina additional stress, as she did not know how to bring her peers together to focus on the company's financial issues. The new team members were requiring more of Elaina's time than she had expected to ensure they understood the company's financial operating model. Other peers expected Elaina to take sides during the arguments.

4. **Sabotage by a peer.**
   Elaina avoided taking sides during the arguments between her peers. She attempted to work individually with each of her peers to create and implement the new financial model. It was difficult to move

things forward when the team was so fractured. As the company's financial situation continued to worsen, one of Elaina's peers began to sabotage her. Her peer told others that the financial difficulties were caused by Elaina's lack of job experience and poor performance as the new CFO. Her peers started to distance themselves from her, and it was hard for her to get time on their calendars to work on the financial issues. Elaina was aware of the sabotage and did not know how to handle it. She knew her peer was complaining to her manager, the CEO, as well. Elaina was concerned about her job, her stress level increased, and it impacted her sleeping habits. She got three to four hours of sleep per night, which affected her ability to focus on the job and eventually affected her health.

Elaina had more than one trigger present in her potential derailment scenario. That made it hard for her to separate and identify all of the issues. Her stress level increased, and her health worsened, and she was unable to pinpoint what had caused her health issues. It took a significant health problem to capture her attention. It is important to become aware of how to improve your habits related to physical, emotional, and spiritual well-being prior to becoming involved in challenging situations. It is essential to take time to evaluate your resiliency strategies and create a Resiliency Action Plan. Below are sample questions based on Elaina's story that can be used to help manage physical, emotional, and spiritual well-being for each of the four derailment triggers. Use these questions as a starting place for creating your action plan, and you can tailor the questions to your personal situation.

DERAILMENT TRIGGER QUESTIONS

To better understand your self-care needs, answer the following questions. These questions will help you to reduce stress and avoid issues associated with derailment.

- How will I close my skill gaps quickly to reduce any stress that lack of job knowledge might create?

- When I become stressed, what type of behaviors do I tend to exhibit that are not beneficial, and what will I do when I recognize I am behaving in a way that is not beneficial?

- What actions do I need to take to build relationships with my new peer team and other stakeholders and gain support for the goals I need to accomplish?

- How will I handle sabotage if it occurs, and what steps can I take to reduce stress if I believe that sabotage is taking place?

- What actions will I take to improve my physical, emotional, and spiritual well-being to increase my energy level and decrease my stress level?

DEFINING 'ENHANCE SELF-CARE'

Enhancing self-care helps you to improve your physical, emotional, and spiritual well-being to increase your energy and decrease stress. To maintain and increase your resiliency, it is important to evaluate your current physical, emotional, and spiritual condition, and then take action to improve those areas that are affecting your well-being. During times of stress at work, it can be easy to forget to focus on healthy habits. Often exercise, diet, and sleep can be overlooked, emotions disregarded, and spiritual activities neglected. A lack of focus on self-care can lead to health issues and an inability to maintain resiliency.

Physical well-being is defined as a combination of exercise, diet, and sleep. Stress can be reduced by engaging in physical activity on a daily basis. Physical activities, such as hiking, biking, walking, strength training, and running, can help increase energy. A well-balanced diet provides the energy needed to focus during stressful conditions and includes certain essential carbohydrates, proteins, fats, vitamins, and minerals. It is important to consume plenty of fluids, including water. Often during stressful conditions, the length and quality of sleep will be disrupted. The body needs rest that can be achieved by relaxing, taking short naps, and getting seven to nine hours of high-quality sleep each night. Lack of sleep can lead to both physical and emotional issues.

Emotional well-being focuses on the mind's emotional state, how you are feeling and expressing those feelings. Emotions can become erratic under stressful conditions, and you may be unaware of how your emotions are being affected or what to do about it. You may lose your temper more frequently at work or home, feel depressed, be unable to focus on the job, and withdraw from social contact. You may engage in negative self-talk, blaming yourself instead of looking at all aspects of the situation. It is important to understand how your emotions are impacted by stress so that you can recognize and address the issues.

The word *spiritual* means something different to everyone. For some, it is defined by their religious beliefs and participation in organized religious traditions. For others, it may mean getting in touch with their spirituality through activities such as private prayer, yoga, meditation, mindfulness, or reflection. Here the definition of spiritual well-being encompasses all those examples of spirituality. During times of stress, it is essential to participate in meaningful activities that keep you in touch with things that boost your spirit or soul, in addition to the physical and emotional. These meaningful activities can help to reduce stress and increase energy. They can enable you to transform and thrive, not just survive challenging situations.

ENHANCE SELF-CARE ACTION STEPS

There are five action steps within *Enhance Self-Care* that you can take to improve your physical, emotional, and spiritual well-being to increase your energy and inoculate yourself against stress:

1. Assess your physical, emotional, and spiritual well-being.

2. Implement actions to improve your physical health.

3. Integrate activities that restore your emotional strength.

4. Incorporate spiritual practices into your schedule.

5. Effectively integrate the time spent on work and self-care activities.

Use the Resiliency Action Plan to create a development plan to improve your physical, emotional, and spiritual well-being. By identifying activities to improve your physical, emotional and spiritual health, creating a Resiliency Action Plan, and making intentional choices about reducing stress and increasing energy, you can successfully manage your career. Resiliency strategies help you thrive when major challenges are happening. Arianna Huffington's story is an example of what can happen when you don't practice self-care. Several years ago, as she was building the Huffington Post, she collapsed due to exhaustion and sleep deprivation.

Her collapse resulted in a broken cheekbone and several stitches near her eye. Following her accident, she realized she had been neglecting her well-being, and she made some significant changes in her life. She began to get more sleep, gradually moving from four to five hours a night to seven to eight hours. Arianna added thirty minutes of meditation to her daily routine, along with yoga or some other form of exercise. She focused on taking a few small steps to decrease stress and increase well-being. Arianna views well-being as a measurement of success.

Arianna not only made changes in her life to enhance self-care, she also made changes at the Huffington Post. To encourage rest and enhance creativity, the Huffington Post introduced nap rooms. The Huffington Post implemented other activities for employees related to physical, emotional, and spiritual well-being, including meditation, yoga, and breathing classes. A focus on eating healthy was introduced that included healthy free snacks. To help employees integrate work and life issues, employees are not expected to be on work email after working hours. When employees are off the job, they are truly off the job. Arianna was quoted as saying, "We used to think that there was a trade-off: You had to sacrifice your professional success in order to achieve inner peace. Now we see, no, not at all."

ENHANCE SELF-CARE: ELAINA'S RESILIENCY ACTION PLAN

Elaina and her husband became very concerned about her health due to her sleeping problems, weight gain, and reoccurring nausea and dizziness. After talking with her doctor, close friends, and her husband, Elaina realized that she needed a stronger focus on her well-being. She had stopped exercising, her diet was poor, she was sleeping only a few hours per night, her emotional state was erratic, and she didn't participate in any activities related to spiritual well-being. Both her physical and mental health were deteriorating, causing problems at work and home. Support from her doctor, friends, and family enabled Elaina to create a Resiliency Action Plan to increase her resiliency and position her for job success in her new role as CFO. Elaina's plan focused on enhancing self-care and included:

- Completing a self-assessment of her perception of the state of her physical, emotional, and spiritual well-being, and including input from others.

- Implementing actions to improve her physical well-being in the areas of exercise, diet, and sleep to lose weight and increase energy.

- Focusing on her emotional well-being to eliminate negative behaviors exhibited when stressed and reduce her negative self-talk.

- Integrating actions related to spiritual well-being that would enable her to cope more effectively with the stress.

- Monitoring her progress on her action plan on an ongoing basis and soliciting feedback from others.

Elaina completed a self-assessment of the state of her physical, emotional, and spiritual well-being, and she rated all three areas as low. She knew she needed to begin working on these areas to reduce stress, increase energy, and feel healthy again. She identified actions to improve her physical well-being. She previously enjoyed walking as her form of exercise, and decided to add that back into her exercise plan. She started walking for one hour on Saturday and Sunday, and added a thirty-minute walk during her lunch hour each day. Elaina knew she needed to make significant changes to her diet. The first step was to eliminate the fast food and replace it with a healthy, well-balanced diet. She believed that improving exercise and diet would enable her to sleep better. To specifically address her sleep deprivation, she stopped working on her computer and watching television two hours before she went to bed.

Elaina realized that the sabotage she experienced had taken a toll on her emotionally, causing her to focus on negative self-talk, including self-blame. She focused actions on how to redirect the negative self-talk and flip the negative to a positive when she heard the self-talk taking place in her mind. Working on her action plan revealed how she had micromanaged her team. She had meetings with each of her direct reports and slowly gave them back tasks to complete that she had owned. She decided to leave work earlier and reduce the amount of time she spent working from home in the evenings and weekends to gain work-life balance.

She was unclear initially on how to proceed with incorporating spiritual activities into her plan. She knew that these types of activities could reduce stress. After doing some research and talking with a close friend, Elaina decided to add meditation and yoga into her weekly routine. She learned that fifteen minutes of meditation a day, and thirty minutes of yoga three to four times a week, could reduce her stress level.

While it wasn't easy to stick with the action plan, Elaina saw immediate results from some of the actions she implemented. The combination of activities enabled her to increase the amount of sleep she was getting. The change in exercise, diet, and sleep resulted in increased energy and ability to focus at work. Her focus on not micromanaging enabled her to delegate more initiatives and spend less time working from home. As a result of dealing with her negative self-talk, she met with the peer who was sabotaging her and had a direct discussion. Incorporating meditation and yoga into her routine led to decreased stress. All these actions together enabled Elaina to successfully help the company turn around its financial performance over time, and succeed in her job as CFO. Because of her focus on her Resiliency Action Plan, Elaina was able to turn around a potentially career-derailing situation.

When you enhance self-care, you make intentional decisions about how to improve your physical, emotional, and spiritual well-being to decrease stress and increase energy. Enhancing self-care can contribute to career success. Elaina put her Resiliency Action Plan in place after the potentially career-derailing experience happened, and she was able to grow and thrive despite the negative experience. She could have implemented the action plan prior to moving into the new role to increase her resiliency and her ability to thrive, not just survive.

ENHANCE SELF-CARE: RESILIENCY ACTION PLAN ACTIVITIES

The purpose of this strategy is to help you determine what steps you need to take to improve your physical, emotional, and spiritual well-being to increase your energy and inoculate yourself against stress. There are five actions that you can take to help you to enhance self-care:

1. Assess your physical, emotional, and spiritual well-being.

2. Implement actions to improve your physical health.

3. Integrate activities that restore your emotional strength.

4. Incorporate spiritual practices into your schedule.

5. Effectively integrate the time spent on work and self-care activities.

Before implementing any activities related to your health, such as exercise or diet, please consult a physician to ensure that you select activities that are appropriate for you. The following five activities will help you take action to enhance self-care.

ACTIVITY 1: ASSESS YOUR PHYSICAL, EMOTIONAL, AND SPIRITUAL WELL-BEING

The purpose of this activity is to complete a self-assessment of your physical, emotional, and spiritual condition. This activity will help you identify areas of improvement in each of the three categories and enable you to create self-care goals for your Resiliency Action Plan. This activity provides you with a framework to assess and identify self-care gaps you want to address.

INSTRUCTIONS

1. Review your self-assessment of Enhance Self-Care in chapter 2. Did you indicate that you were thriving, surviving, or declining when it came to self-care?

2. Complete the self-assessment below (**Table 10.1**) for each of the categories within Enhance Self-Care to determine the specific areas you need to focus on for your action plan. Place an X in Thriving, Surviving, or Declining for each well-being category.

   Record your results from the self-assessment and refer to your Resiliency Action Plan Summary Worksheet (**Table 10.5**) at the end of this chapter. Your results from this self-assessment will be used to complete Activities 2, 3, and 4.

Table 10.1

ENHANCE SELF-CARE SELF-ASSESSMENT WORKSHEET			
WELL-BEING/ RATING	THRIVING	SURVIVING	DECLINING
PHYSICAL EXERCISE	Exercises regularly 4–5 days a week, both cardio and strength training	Exercises sporadically 2–3 days a week, strength and/or cardio	Exercises rarely, if at all
PHYSICAL DIET	Regularly eats a well-balanced diet; no significant unintentional weight gain or loss	Sometimes eats a well-balanced diet; may have unexpectedly gained or lost weight	Rarely eats a well-balanced diet; has unexpectedly gained or lost weight
PHYSICAL SLEEP	Gets 7–8 hours of uninterrupted sleep each night	Gets 5–6 hours of sleep each night; may have some interruptions	Gets 3–4 hours of sleep per night or less; frequently interrupted
EMOTIONAL	Emotions are not erratic, and rarely any negative self-talk or blame	Emotions may sometimes be erratic and/or some negative self-talk or blame	Emotions are frequently erratic along with negative self-talk and blame
SPIRITUAL	Engages regularly in 1–2 spiritual well-being activities 4–5 times a week	Engages sporadically in 1 spiritual well-being activity 1–2 times a week	Rarely engages in spiritual well-being activities

ACTIVITY 2: IMPLEMENT ACTIONS TO IMPROVE YOUR PHYSICAL HEALTH

This activity will enable you to create SMART goals to enhance your physical well-being. Physical well-being goals will be different for every individual, depending on the gaps that need to be addressed and the individual's preferred mode of exercise. Daily exercise, diet, and sleep are important to maintain physical health, decrease stress, and increase energy.

INSTRUCTIONS

1. Create the following table (**Table 10.2**) by transferring your self-assessment rating from Activity 1 (**Table 10.1**), physical well-being, to a table similar to the one below.

2. For each physical well-being category that you rated as surviving or declining, write a SMART goal that will enable you to reduce stress, increase energy, and thrive. An example of a SMART goal is: *Power walk for four miles, four days a week, to increase cardio activity and lose ten pounds.*

Table 10.2

Well-Being/Rating	Thriving	Surviving	Declining
Physical—Exercise			
SMART Goal			
Physical—Diet			
SMART Goal			
Physical—Sleep			
SMART Goal			

Create your SMART goals for physical well-being and refer to your Resiliency Action Plan Summary Worksheet (**Table 10.5**) at the end of this chapter.

ACTIVITY 3: INTEGRATE ACTIVITIES THAT RESTORE YOUR EMOTIONAL STRENGTH

This activity enables you to create specific goals to improve how you manage your emotions during times of stress, including negative self-talk. Emotional well-being focuses on the mind's emotional state, how you are feeling and expressing those feelings. Your action plan may include goals to reduce negative self-talk or to better understand your emotions and the impact they have on you. It is important to understand how your emotions are affected by stress so that you can recognize and address the issues.

INSTRUCTIONS

1. Create the following table (**Table 10.3**) by transferring your self-assessment rating from Activity 1 (**Table 10.1**), emotional well-being, to a table similar to the one below.

Table 10.3

Well-Being/Rating	Thriving	Surviving	Declining
Emotional			
SMART Goal(s)			

2. If you rated emotional well-being as surviving or declining, write a SMART goal that will enable you to reduce stress, increase energy, and thrive. You may write more than one SMART goal. An example of a SMART goal is: *Write negative self-talk in my journal on the day it happens and then write a positive version to replace the negative self-*

talk. Replace the negative message with the positive message each time I say it to myself.

   Create your SMART goal for emotional well-being and refer to your Resiliency Action Plan Summary Worksheet (**Table 10.5**) at the end of this chapter.

ACTIVITY 4: INCORPORATE SPIRITUAL PRACTICES INTO YOUR SCHEDULE

This activity will help you to create specific goals to enhance your spiritual well-being. The activities included in spiritual well-being will vary based upon the individual. Your action plan may include religion, private prayer, yoga, meditation, mindfulness, or reflection, depending on your preferences. During times of stress, it is essential to participate in meaningful activities that keep you in touch with things that affect your spirit or soul.

INSTRUCTIONS

1. Create the following table (**Table 10. 4**) by transferring your self-assessment rating from Activity 1, (**Table 10.1**) spiritual well-being, to a table similar to the one below.

Table 10.4

Well-Being/Rating	Thriving	Surviving	Declining
Spiritual			
SMART Goal(s)			

2. If you rated spiritual well-being as surviving or declining, write a SMART goal that will enable you to reduce stress, increase energy, and thrive. You may write more than one SMART goal. An example of a SMART goal is: *Meditate in the morning for 30 minutes, five times a week, to reduce stress.*

Create your SMART goals for spiritual well-being and refer to your Resiliency Action Plan Summary Worksheet (**Table 10.5**) at the end of this chapter.

ACTIVITY 5: *EFFECTIVELY INTEGRATE THE TIME SPENT ON WORK AND SELF-CARE ACTIVITIES*

This activity will provide you with information about your perception of your work and life integration. It will help you to track how the action items you have implemented are affecting your physical, emotional, and spiritual well-being. You may believe your work and life are effectively integrated, but asking the question regularly will help you to adjust your work and self-care activities and implement additional action plans as needed to achieve integration.

INSTRUCTIONS

1. Create your work and life integration scale indicator by identifying how you will know what it looks like to function at a "one" (work and life are not integrated) or a "ten" (work and life are highly integrated). What will you think or feel when you're at either end of the continuum? How will you behave? What will people say to you?

2. If you are journaling, decide if you want to include this activity in your journal or track it separately in your Resiliency Action Plan.

3. Set up calendar reminders to ask yourself at the end of each day if work and life were effectively integrated that day, on a scale of one to ten. You may also want to look back at the Resiliency Action Plan at the end of each week and ask if your work and life were integrated that week.

4. Write down the number you selected in your journal if you are journaling, or in your Resiliency Action Plan. Make notes about

why you selected that number. What thoughts did you have that caused your work and life integration indicator number to be high or low? How did your focus on physical, emotional, and spiritual well-being affect your work and life integration?

5. Take the time to reflect each day on your work and life integration indicator and explore why it is high or low. Make notes about what makes your life more or less integrated. Regularly update your self-care SMART goals on your Resiliency Action Plan. Replicate those activities that give you a high work and life integration indicator.

 Create one SMART goal to increase your work and life integration score and refer to your Resiliency Action Plan Summary Worksheet at the end of this chapter.

RESILIENCY ACTION PLAN SUMMARY WORKSHEET

Refer to the worksheet (**Table 10.5**) to summarize key outcomes and SMART goals from the activities in this chapter.

For each activity associated with this strategy, make sure you have identified a key outcome or SMART goal to help you take action. Capture these commitments in your day planner or calendar to ensure that you complete them.

Table 10.5

☑	Resiliency Action Plan Summary Worksheet
Activity	**Key Outcome or SMART Goals**
1	
2	
3	
4	
5	

ADDITIONAL RESOURCES

The following resources may consist of online videos, apps, and assessment tools that could provide greater depth on key concepts associated with this Resiliency Strategy. We have no control over and do not endorse third-party content, goods, or services.

- H.A.L.T.—A Tool For Self Care (Online Video, 11 minutes). Four useful tips to be your best self. Available at https://youtu.be/lXagULcrrBg.

- Relax Melodies (App). Soothing sounds to help you increase your self-care by getting better sleep. Available at http://www.ipnossoft.com.

- Self-Care is Selfish—NOT (Online Video, 1 minute). Powerful inspirational video with affirmations for women. Available at https://www.youtube.com/watch?v=-hbc87ilMZI.

ELEVEN

RUCHIKA'S STORY: ON THE EDGE OF THE CAREER CLIFF

BY RUCHIKA TULSHYAN

My mission in life is not merely to survive, but to thrive; and to do so with some passion, some compassion, some humor, and some style.
— Maya Angelou

The first five years after graduating from college, I lived my career dream. I worked in four countries: the United Kingdom, Singapore, India (Mumbai), and the United States. The jobs provided me with exciting challenges in the field of communications. I learned new skills and developed my professional capabilities. In my late twenties, I started a new job as a marketing manager at a fast-growing start-up in the United States. It was one of the most challenging roles I had worked in because of a fast-paced environment and a requirement to learn new technology on the fly. I was working with some of the smartest people I had ever met. It was exhilarating. I could see a future for my career in this organization.

Then, for the first time in my career, I encountered a situation that I was not prepared to handle. Several months after starting my new job, a senior leader expressed dissatisfaction with my performance and suggested that I should be fired. I didn't understand what I had done, and I was devastated because I had been working hard at excelling in this new area of communications. Suddenly, I felt like I was on the edge of the career cliff, about to be pushed off. It was frightening.

Four months after beginning my new job, I was assigned to work closely with the senior leader who later questioned my performance and attitude. This leader did not directly manage me. I was excited to be working with someone with such strong expertise in the profession. We worked closely together on developing communication strategies for the company. I reached out to this leader and shared my ideas frequently, as I had been invited to do. After several weeks of working together, no concerns had been expressed directly to me about my outreach or work performance.

Around this same time, my manager scheduled a meeting with me. The senior leader had told my manager and a senior executive that I was difficult to work with, and that it would be best to let me go. When I told my manager that I would like to discuss the issue with the discontented senior leader, I was told not to have that discussion. I had been working with my manager for a while, so I knew that this was a significant issue, since my organization was very casual and non-hierarchical. My intuition told me that something was very wrong and that I wasn't being told the entire story. I forced myself to be professional.

My manager said he would reach out to three other senior leaders I had interacted with, for feedback on what it was like to work with me. While my boss reiterated I was a great employee with an impressive track record, he felt it necessary to verify this with other leaders. I somehow remained calm for the rest of the day, but as soon as I walked out of the office that evening, I couldn't hold back the tears. I was so shaken up. I couldn't understand the reason for the negative feedback and wondered why the senior leader hadn't provided the feedback directly to me. Although I didn't know what I did wrong and I apparently wouldn't find out, I was tasked with having to prove myself. I had to validate myself as a better worker and as a better person. I was so surprised, because I had received consistent feedback that I was a professional and pleasant coworker. I spent the next few weeks pondering whether it would be better for me to quit my job.

To decide if I should quit my job, I first reached out to my support networks. I asked for advice on whether to resign and for objective opinions on my supposed difficulties in working with others. I reached out to my mother for emotional support. I called upon former colleagues and mentors who had championed me. It was important for me to become more self-aware and get an independent view about what I was doing well and my areas for improvement.

This became especially important in the first few weeks after the incident, since senior members of my organization scrutinized me. On one hand, I had to maintain a professional and cheerful demeanor; on the other, I had to work doubly hard to prove myself and deliver outstanding results. It was valuable to enlist the help of mentors, who reminded me that my work naturally spoke for itself. My mentors also challenged me to work on getting myself to an emotional state where I felt authentic at work. It helped tremendously to have an emotional support network that I could turn to during moments when I felt low.

I wanted to build my self-awareness and identify what made me unique. The negative feedback felt like a personal attack, and I initially felt compelled to blame myself and change my behaviors. Through self-reflection and my group of mentors, I was reminded that it was my tenacity that had gotten me so far in my career. I always raised my hand and voiced my thoughts, and my mentors suggested I shouldn't think I needed to change these behaviors due to this negative incident. I needed help making the decision on whether to quit. I enjoyed my job and my team, but working with someone who sent me such mixed signals created one of the most difficult work environments I had ever been in. I needed to take some time to clarify my purpose, to focus on what I wanted from my life. I wrote down a list of the pros and cons of my job. I had used this tactic in the past to help me make important decisions.

Apart from a long commute and dealing with the trauma of this experience, I was happy with my job. It would take some time to align myself with my career goals after this setback, but that became my focus. My mentors also repeatedly advised me not to give up on this job, because I enjoyed the work and would be successful if I made it through this challenge. During this time, I learned a great deal about how to manage myself, and I developed new behaviors, including soliciting feedback and listening carefully before speaking. When my manager asked other senior team members their opinions of me, I was initially mortified, and yet it turned out to be a great validation of my hard work to date. It also renewed my optimism and purpose for working at the company. I decided I would continue being myself.

I took advantage of the weekly meetings I had with my manager to ask for honest feedback about my job performance and my behaviors, something I hadn't done before. With this feedback, I became more metrics and data-driven. The company's culture was data-focused, and I used numbers to support my performance. After this incident, I purposefully started using metrics to track my goals and performance until it became a habit. It's one new habit that has since helped me achieve many other career and personal goals.

The hardest part for me was managing my emotional reactions to the senior leader who had caused me so much anguish. I knew that a confrontation would not be helpful, and I didn't want to circumvent my manager's request. I consciously made a choice to treat the senior leader with respect, while carefully avoiding interactions that weren't critical. In the meantime, I continued building relationships with other team members and worked hard to prove myself.

This incident caused me to reflect deeply on my attitudes. I asked myself if I was too forceful or pushy with my ideas. While my mentors didn't mention this as an area of improvement, I took it upon myself to listen carefully and think more before speaking. I didn't retreat or stop sharing ideas, but I learned to share them more thoughtfully. Slowly but intentionally, I built up my confidence and raised my hand to lead some big projects in my department. I ensured I was visible and collaborative with a variety of people in the company.

Within six months, my manager and I were talking about my getting a raise and promotion. It felt great to have him say that I was excelling so quickly that I deserved a raise. I received a departmental award for achieving a target that directly impacted our bottom line. At that moment I felt as if I had emerged powerful and strong from a big storm. The experience had me thinking about my long-term life goals. Over time, I knew that the workplace environment wasn't right for me. I started realizing that the leaders of the organization preferred not to tackle tough issues about employee engagement and let resentment simmer under the surface. The experience confirmed something I had been writing about for years as a career journalist focused on diversity. Many companies seem ill-equipped to champion diversity and foster a culture that rewards collaboration and mutual support.

I began to realize that my purpose in life had shifted, and though I was a few short months away from being promoted, I wasn't fulfilled by my job. I decided it was time to leave my corporate job about eight months after the incident occurred. It was time for me to focus on my passion and write a book on how organizations can build gender-balanced workplaces. In my last week of work, I found out that the senior leader who had caused me so much pain had left the organization. But that did not change my decision to leave. I had not just survived, but thrived, in the face of adversity, and I had become a better person because of it. I was able to learn how to successfully fly off the edge of the career cliff. Listed below are my suggestions for thriving when dealing with workplace challenges.

- Identify mentors who can challenge you and help you develop. It was only by identifying and calling upon my social network that I was able to regain the confidence I had lost through this experience.

- Reflect periodically on how well you are using and actualizing your strengths. My initial reaction was to quit, thinking I had failed and had no strengths. But in reality, I needed to reflect on what made me unique and how I could leverage those strengths to be more effective.

- Make conscious choices about your reactions to others. My immediate reaction was to confront and resolve the situation amicably. I eventually learned that the answer lies in controlling your reactions, and that not every tough situation can be resolved through communication.

- Embrace a growth mindset in facing your challenges. I was able to develop new skills that have helped me in my career far beyond this one experience.

- Reframe negative situations to find the silver lining. Without this experience, it would have taken me longer to find my true calling and purpose, which is to write my book.

Biography

Ruchika Tulshyan is the author of *The Diversity Advantage: Fixing Gender Inequality in the Workplace* (Forbes, 2015). Her writing focuses on diversity and leadership. She has been published in *Forbes*, the *Wall Street Journal*, and Bloomberg. Ruchika is originally from Singapore, and has lived in six cities across three continents. In her spare time, she loves to cook and travel. You can follow Ruchika on Twitter @rtulshyan and contact her at rtulshyan@gmail.com.

TWELVE

RESILIENCY STRATEGY: ACTUALIZE STRENGTHS

Maximize your strengths to build confidence, gain the courage to take risks, and achieve greater results.

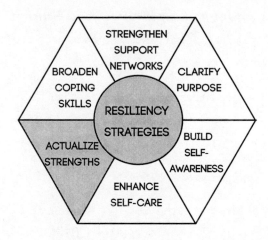

Personal power comes from a deep awareness and reverence for the strengths that make us unique. These strengths are a part of our physical wiring and yearn to be expressed.
— KEVIN NOURSE

ACTUALIZE STRENGTHS: LIN'S STORY

Lin was close to fulfilling her dream of launching a business. Her employer, a large global company, merged with a competitor and experienced a downsizing. Employees were given the option to volunteer to be laid off and receive a generous severance package. Lin had long dreamed of starting her technology consulting business, but had never managed to develop a business plan. Despite not having a written business plan, Lin volunteered to give up her job, accept a generous severance package, and pursue her lifelong desire to start her own business. The first ten months in business were very successful as a result of landing a major contract with a large company. However, an unexpected leadership transition within her client organization led to the cancellation of her projects.

In her former role, Lin was a highly successful web developer and systems analyst. After graduating with a degree in information technology, she joined her employer ten years ago. Her analytical ability, passion for technology, and introverted personality were a great fit for her software developer role. However, Lin was afraid of conflict with authority figures and never pushed back on her manager when he gave her new assignments, even when they were a bad fit for her strengths and interests. As a result, she often felt unqualified, which prompted her to work even harder on stretch assignments. Although the job was not perfect, Lin was happy to work for a company with such generous benefits and a convenient commute.

After her employer announced the merger and downsizing, Lin jumped at the chance to launch her business. She reached out to one of her former colleagues who had launched a consulting business several years prior. He was very convincing about the benefits of self-employment, prompting Lin to conclude that this could be a great next step in her career. Lin submitted a request to be downsized to her manager, and it was approved. Two weeks after leaving her job, Lin launched her web consulting business and rented office space in a nearby office park. She felt excited as well as terrified for taking such a bold step in her career. Within weeks after leaving her employer, a colleague she knew in her former role introduced Lin to her husband, who needed a consultant to help advance some large projects. The combination of Lin's discomfort with asking for what she wanted and self-doubt about her abilities caused her to substantially underprice her proposal. She quickly landed the contract with his company because of her expertise as well as the low rate she proposed. Her contact assured her that the project would last at least two years. Lin was elated with this opportunity and began to feel like she could succeed at self-employment.

Her initial euphoria at winning the client project was diminished once she realized how much work the projects would entail. Lin developed a work plan to complete the necessary tasks her client needed by the first milestone date. While it was overwhelming, she believed she could do it all if she worked at nights and on the weekend. Although her skills meshed well with some of the tasks she was assigned, several tasks required skills she did not have. Lin mistakenly believed if she worked longer and harder, she could learn while producing the results expected by her client. Unfortunately, she missed a major deadline with her client as a result. Fortunately, the client contact was very forgiving and extended the deadline. Lin realized the only way she could complete these tasks on time was to find web developers to help her. Through her former colleagues, she identified and hired three senior software developers to help her fulfill the contract in the time frame her client wanted.

All three of her employees were experienced software developers who were highly skilled with the technology used by her client. Although the addition of three new staff allowed her to meet the expectations of her client, she initially struggled in her new role managing the work of others. Lin's passion for and experience with software development resulted in her telling her staff in excruciating detail how to perform their roles. Rather than focus on other aspects of running her fledgling business, Lin micromanaged her direct reports. At first, this was not an issue, and her developers deferred to her. However, after several weeks one of her most qualified developers met with Lin, indicated the job was not working out, and resigned. Lin was shocked to realize he was so dissatisfied with his role. After talking for an hour, he finally revealed that her micromanaging leadership style was the primary reason for his dissatisfaction. Lin felt defensive about his feedback and decided that his leaving might actually be the best outcome. She decided to reallocate the remaining projects between her two other developers and pay closer attention to their morale.

Despite ten successful months working with this client, Lin received some unexpected information about the project. The CEO of her client organization resigned, and the new CEO hired his executive team. As a result, all of the major information technology projects, including the one she was engaged to complete, were placed on hold indefinitely until the new chief information officer could formulate his strategy. Lin received a call one Friday afternoon from her primary contact informing her of the bad news. He explained that it had nothing to do with the quality of her work and everything to do with the internal politics and leadership transitions of his company. Lin felt deeply disappointed because of the earlier assurance she had received about the long-term nature of the project. Because of this assurance and her disdain for marketing, she had done little to reach out to other prospective clients. The expectation of a long-term contract led her to hire three people, rent a beautiful office, and make costly investments in computer equipment. She struggled with what to do now and felt pangs of anxiety as she thought about the lack of cash coming into the business.

With her only client project placed on hold and no backup projects in the marketing pipeline, Lin began to struggle to stay afloat financially. She had inadequate financial resources to ride this downturn because of the cost of her staff and office space, as well as the low rate she was billing the client. Because of Lin's passion for software development and her discomfort with marketing, she had not invested time in developing other client options. Lin met with her accountant, who advised her that she would be out of cash within three months if she did not immediately reduce her expenses or bring in new revenue sources. She left the meeting feeling her heart racing, unsure of what to do to address the situation. Lin realized that she had assumed that her technical knowledge and strong reputation would be enough to ensure the success of her business.

The next couple of weeks were emotionally draining as Lin attempted to revitalize her business. In her attempts to conserve cash, Lin decided she could not afford the two remaining staff as well as her contract accountant. Her initial attempts to manage her finances as well as develop new business did not go well. She priced her work too low and had a difficult time clearly explaining her qualifications. Lin submitted one proposal for a software development project based on a request for a proposal she received. While Lin had experience using the technologies requested by the client, her skills had rapidly grown outdated. When the technology director called her to discuss the proposal and explore her credentials, not only did her skills lack currency, but her self-doubt prevented her from promoting her other qualifications. As a result, she did not win the project. Even though she did not have an accounting background, she attempted to manage her business financials and made several mistakes, resulting in being overdrawn on her business checking account.

Lin began to doubt her decision to attempt self-employment. She realized that the persuasive personality of her former colleague caused her to launch her business without the necessary planning and preparation. Lin felt embarrassed at her failure and avoided her former colleagues, who often asked about her business. As a result, she began reluctantly reviewing the online job search sites to find a full-time position.

DERAILMENT TRIGGERS

Lin's story contains some critical derailment triggers that likely contributed to and deepened the painful experience she endured:

1. **Mismatched personality for the job role.**
   Lin made the mistake of choosing self-employment without considering whether she had the right personality to create a sustainable business. The ability to market your skills and cope

with uncertainty is just as important as technical skill. Some people function well as entrepreneurs, while others desire a well-defined job in an organizational setting.

2. **Overusing one's strengths.**

Lin made the mistake of overusing her strength for software development and tending to details that contributed to micromanaging her staff. In many cases, strengths can become a liability when they are overused or used in the wrong situation.

3. **Undervaluing one's strengths.**

Lin made a classic mistake of entrepreneurs in underpricing herself because of a lack of confidence in her abilities and a lack of awareness of the value of her strengths. She also overlooked her core strengths as she attempted to chase after potential business for which she was not qualified and perform accounting tasks that diverted her focus from developing crucial client relationships. As a result, she wasted time pursuing business leads that did not pay off.

4. **Not developing one's strengths.**

Lin made the mistake of focusing so much on her current projects that she did not set aside time to develop her core strengths. As a result, she became less marketable. Strengths are like any asset, and need to be maintained to ensure they are viable.

Each of the derailment triggers in Lin's story can either be avoided or minimized through proactive reflection and action.

DERAILMENT TRIGGER QUESTIONS

In light of the derailment triggers identified in Lin's story, there are several useful questions to reflect on as a way to prevent adversity in your career:

- To what extent do your strengths match the core requirements of your role?

- How clear are you about your professional strengths? How confident are you in communicating your strengths to others?

- To what extent do you overuse your strengths?

- How willing are you to leverage others' strengths to augment your weaknesses?

- How clear are you on how to develop your strengths? How much time do you spend focusing on your development?

By asking yourself these questions in advance, you can anticipate potential career challenges, consider your options for coping with them, and ensure you maintain your resiliency.

DEFINING 'ACTUALIZE STRENGTHS'

Actualizing your strengths enables you to build confidence, gain the courage to take risks, and achieve greater results. Strengths represent a combination of innate talent and conceptual knowledge, skill, and wisdom. Knowing and valuing your strengths leads you to internalize your sense of power and feel confident. When people feel confident, they are more likely to assert their ideas and achieve success, shape their environment, and feel more in control of their destiny. Those who doubt their strengths often overcompensate, causing them to overuse their ability, which leads to negative effects on their performance and reputation.

A key driver of assertiveness is feeling powerful in the form of confidence. Confidence comes from a deep regard for your skills, abilities, and other factors that make you unique. It represents a deep sense of belief in yourself and your abilities. People who have positive self-regard have a grounded perspective on their abilities and are neither too modest about their strengths nor too boastful. Confidence is manifest in your words and nonverbal body language. People who demonstrate confidence and conviction in their words, gestures, style of speaking, and other nonverbal behaviors have leadership presence.

Your strengths should be evaluated and developed to ensure they remain viable and current. Since strengths consist of innate talent, as well as skills and knowledge, they must be developed to ensure they are sustained. For example, some people have an innate talent for connecting with others, and they demonstrate it in the way they easily make friends, connect people, and socialize. This talent, combined with conceptual knowledge about team dynamics and observable skills such as facilitating a meeting, contributes to the demonstration of the strength. People who have this strength can develop and sustain it by reading recent research on group dynamics, practicing new skills in helping a group navigate conflict, or inviting a colleague to observe them and provide feedback.

Another aspect of developing your strengths involves knowing how frequently or when to use them. When strengths are overused or used in the wrong situation, they can become a liability. For example, a facilitator who asks too many probing questions in a group meeting to challenge participants can trigger defensiveness and destroy trust. Resilient people are aware of their strengths and invest energy in developing them that could include enhancing their knowledge, skill, or building situational awareness of when to use them.

ACTUALIZE STRENGTHS ACTION STEPS

There are five action steps within *Actualize Strengths* that can be taken to help you actualize your strengths and enable you to build confidence, gain the courage to take risks, and achieve greater results:

1. Identify your unique strengths.

2. Determine ways to use your strengths more fully on a regular basis.

3. Identify others who can augment your weaknesses.

4. Find ways to develop your strengths.

5.   Identify other key factors that help you feel confident and powerful.

You can use the Resiliency Action Plan to help actualize your strengths. By actualizing your strengths, you will build confidence and take risks, thereby achieving greater results in your career.

Camilla Bowry is a social entrepreneur who was nominated for a prestigious award by the Asian Women of Achievement in the Social and Humanitarian category for her work as the founder of Sal's Shoes. Her nonprofit organization collects and redistributes pre-loved children's shoes. In the first year of operation, Bowry's organization distributed nearly 5,000 pairs of shoes to children in eight countries. Her idea for this organization came out of her inability to find a suitable organization to which she could donate the shoes no longer worn by her son Sal. Bowry discovered that millions of barefoot children around the world are at higher risk of disease and injury. Without shoes, they are also unable to attend school in many countries and must pay for their education. Once she communicated her plans for providing shoes to disadvantaged children, Camilla was overwhelmed with the volume of contributions from friends and family. This response led her to create an organization to support the demand; thus Sal's Shoes was born.

Her role as CEO and founder is an ideal fit for her strengths, personality, experience, and education. Born in the United Kingdom, she lived in Africa as a child after her father relocated the family for his work as a civil engineer. She went on to study social anthropology and development before working in the elderly care sector, and then gaining entrepreneurial experience helping to manage her husband's property development business after the birth of her first child. These strengths, combined with her talent for multitasking, her efficiency in time management, and her ability to work well under pressure have helped create many early successes in growing her organization. By the end of the second year of Sal's Shoes, over 25,000 pairs of outgrown shoes had been collected and redistributed in 18 countries. Bowry noted in an interview how she has no qualms in asking for help and has "always asked for support and guidance from others" to augment aspects of running Sal's Shoes. For example, in the early days of launching Sal's Shoes, she realized the need to establish a brand and social media presence to communicate her story. Without hesitating, she reached out to a friend who was a graphics designer to enlist his help in creating a logo. Bowry took the same approach to augment her lack of certain information technology skills by engaging friends who had social media and web development experience. With the influx of unsolicited offers of support from large companies interested in partnering with her organization, Bowry recognizes that she may need additional financial expertise to help her navigate these new challenges.

ACTUALIZE STRENGTHS: LIN'S RESILIENCY ACTION PLAN

Lin realized that the challenges she faced in launching her business and the lack of progress in resolving them meant she needed to rethink her career direction. Her efforts to perform all the tasks needed to operate the business with no solid results led her to assess her core strengths and other factors that made her unique. She studied past performance evaluations, asked for input from former colleagues and internal customers from her prior role, and created a list of peak experiences in her professional life. This analysis helped her realize that some of her key strengths included defining user software requirements, creativity in designing the user interfaces on applications, and software coding. Her big insight came when she realized that marketing, public speaking, and business planning were not on her list of strengths. With this information, she was able to focus on her strong areas in how she marketed her abilities to clients or future employers. Lin also took some time to think about her lack of self-confidence and assertiveness. She realized that by internalizing her strengths and preparing for tough conversations by identifying the desired outcome, she could be more effective in asking for what she wanted.

While she appreciated the freedom and sense of self-determination that comes with owning a business, the need to constantly market her services to prospective clients was very unappealing. After talking with several self-employed professional contacts, Lin realized that a better path might be subcontracting to entrepreneurial information technology consulting businesses. She was more than willing to forgo a higher hourly rate for the prospect of steady subcontracting assignments where someone else did the marketing for her. By taking such a role, she could focus on using her strengths and stabilizing her financial situation. Her colleagues helped her identify the names of contacts with several consulting organizations that looked like a good match for her skills and style.

This new approach would lessen her risk and allow her to explore self-employment in a more sustainable way. Lin also identified some professional associations for information technology professionals that offered an extensive catalog of continuing education classes. Because it had been several years since she attended a class, her strengths were diminished and this limited her ability to market herself. As she participated in these programs, she increased her confidence and learned of new consulting opportunities through contacts she made with other participants.

As a result of the changes Lin made, she began feeling more grounded and confident in herself and her career direction. After several months in her new subcontracting role, she had created several deliverables that were very well received by her client. This success helped Lin realize that she could ask for a higher rate for her services. Because she spent the bulk of her workdays leveraging her strengths, she came home energized and began to explore more of her passions beyond her work. Lin felt more satisfied in her life and more optimistic about her future. In looking back at her frustrated attempts to start a business, Lin reframed the painful experience as a growth experience and felt grateful for how much she had grown from the challenges she faced.

ACTUALIZE STRENGTHS: RESILIENCY ACTION PLAN ACTIVITIES

The purpose of this strategy is to help you strengthen the skills necessary to reframe the challenge and make intentional choices that lead to growth and thriving, not just surviving. There are five action steps that you can take to help actualize your strengths:

1. Identify your unique strengths.

2. Determine ways to use your strengths more fully on a regular basis.

3. Identify others who can augment your weaknesses.

4. Find ways to develop your strengths.

5. Identify other key factors that help you feel confident and powerful.

The following five activities will help you take action to actualize your strengths.

ACTIVITY 1: IDENTIFY YOUR UNIQUE STRENGTHS

In this activity, you will be asked to identify your unique strengths based on a review of peak experiences, performance evaluations, and the perceptions of trusted allies and contacts. By inventorying your strengths, you will be better equipped to assert your ideas confidently when you face challenging situations.

INSTRUCTIONS

1. Refer to the Strengths Inventory Worksheet (**Table 12.1**) and identify strengths from three sources, including performance evaluations, peak experiences, and trusted colleagues who are familiar with your work:

Table 12.1

Strengths Inventory Worksheet								
Strengths	Perf. Evaluations		Peak Experiences			Feedback from Colleagues			Total
	1	2	1	2	3	1	2	3	

a. Find and review two performance evaluations from your current or past job roles. In determining how much consideration to give to this feedback, reflect on the reputation of your manager and the extent to which they based their opinions on your actual performance. Capture strengths identified in the evaluation in the first column on the worksheet.

b. Reflect on each of three peak professional experiences and actions you took to achieve these positive outcomes. For example, if you successfully managed a large project that met your customer's requirements that was completed on time and under budget, you would capture project management as one of your strengths. If these strengths were not identified in part a, capture them.

c. Identify three trusted colleagues who would be willing to provide feedback on your strengths. Interview each of them and probe their insights on your strengths. For each strength identified by your colleagues, review the first column, and if you do not already have it listed, add it to the column. Examples of useful questions to ask include:

   • Can you recall a time I achieved excellent results?
   • What strengths did I demonstrate to achieve this success?
   • What was the impact of these strengths?

2. After identifying a list of strengths in the first column, place a checkmark in the subsequent columns if that strength was identified by the specific source. For example, if you identified project management as a strength in the first column, place a checkmark in the performance evaluation #1 column if that strength was identified by that source. Continue across the worksheet columns, placing checkmarks in each column where the strength was identified.

3. Total the number of checks in each row. Sort the list by total number of checks and list your top five strengths below:
   a. Strength #1:
   b. Strength #2:
   c. Strength #3:
   d. Strength #4:
   e. Strength #5:

 Refer to the Resiliency Action Plan Summary Worksheet (**Table 12.6**) at the end of this chapter, capture your top five strengths, and write a SMART goal to validate your newly discovered strengths. For example: *I will validate my list of top five strengths with three colleagues by the end of the month.*

ACTIVITY 2: DETERMINE WAYS TO USE YOUR STRENGTHS MORE FULLY ON A REGULAR BASIS

Now that you have identified your key strengths in Activity 1, it is critical to find ways to use them on a regular basis. By doing so, you will continue to strengthen them, create value for others, and feel more satisfied. Ideally, you can use all of your strengths in your professional role. However, a volunteer role may be a more effective way to use some of your strengths if your current professional role does not provide this opportunity. For example, assume you are currently working in information technology but have an unused strength for developing and empowering people.

Perhaps you could use this talent in your professional role in several ways:

- Mentoring and coaching new employees in your department.

- Moving into a supervisory position that includes the ability to coach and develop your subordinates.

- Volunteering for cross-functional committees in your organization focused on staff morale, retention, or development.

- Helping to facilitate a new hire orientation for new staff.

Further, you could also consider exploring volunteer roles to leverage your strength:

- Volunteering for a crisis telephone hotline service.

- Volunteering to become a Big Sister or Big Brother to a needy child.

- Getting involved in the professional association for information technology and mentoring new people in the profession.

INSTRUCTIONS

1. Complete the Strengths Usage Worksheet (**Table 12.2**):
   a. List your five key strengths.
   b. List ways that you are using each strength in your current professional role.
   c. Brainstorm additional ways you can use your strengths in your current role.
   d. Brainstorm potential ways to use your strengths in a new role that you could propose to your manager.
   e. Brainstorm ways you might use your strengths in a volunteer organization, such as community service or a professional association.

Table 12.2

Strengths Usage Worksheet				
	Professional			Volunteer
Strengths	Current Use	Potential Use Existing Role	Potential Use New Role	Potential Use New Role

Refer to the Resiliency Action Plan Summary Worksheet (**Table 12.6**) at the end of this chapter and write a SMART goal to use your strengths more frequently. For example: *I will discuss with my manager ways I can more frequently use one of my key strengths by June 15.*

ACTIVITY 3: IDENTIFY OTHERS WHO CAN AUGMENT YOUR WEAKNESSES

Rather than trying to be all things to all people, resilient people focus on using their strengths and leveraging the abilities of others to augment their weaknesses. Building upon Activity 2, you will have an opportunity in this activity to reflect on a challenge or goal and identify people who can augment your weaknesses.

For example, let's assume you are interested in leaving your organization and starting a business. Specific skills or abilities you might need to launch your business include marketing, finance, time management, public speaking, project management, and customer management. A good way to determine the skills needed in a new role involves information interviews with people who are currently functioning in your target role. Perhaps you are skilled in managing projects and customers but lack the strengths to perform the other roles. It is important to identify others who could augment your weaknesses and provide support for the other capabilities needed. You might identify paid resources such as an accountant, or a low- or no-cost supporter, such as an intern or a colleague with whom you exchange services.

INSTRUCTIONS

1. Complete the Leveraging the Strengths of Others Worksheet (**Table 12.3**):

    a. Identify and describe a specific challenge or goal you face in your career, or the job to which you aspire.

    b. Identify and list the specific skills or abilities that are needed to address this challenge. To complete this list, you could consult with trusted colleagues or friends who can help you think about your challenge or goal.

    c. Place a check in the second column if the skill or ability needed is one of your strengths.

    d. For those skills or abilities that are not strengths, brainstorm the roles of people who could support you and specific names if they come to mind.

Table 12.3

Leveraging the Strengths of Others Worksheet			
Career Challenge or Goal:			
Skills Needed	Your Strength?	Others to Leverage	
		Role	Name

2. Review your support network to find the names of individuals who can fulfill each of the roles you have identified.

3. Consider the possibility of hiring people to provide the skill or ability needed, bartering to exchange your strengths, or engaging an intern who has strengths you can tap.

 Refer to the Resiliency Action Plan Summary Worksheet (**Table 12.6**) at the end of this chapter and write a SMART goal to leverage others' strengths. For example: *By January 30*

I will enlist the support of a key stakeholder to help me with the specific challenge I'm facing.

ACTIVITY 4: FIND WAYS TO DEVELOP YOUR STRENGTHS

Resilient people continually develop their strengths to sustain their performance and achieve even greater levels of success. In this activity, you will focus on your top five strengths and create a plan for their development. For example, assume one of your strengths is project management. To develop this strength, you might consider:

- Increasing your knowledge by reading professional project management journals on a monthly basis.

- Enhancing your skill by taking a class on the latest project management software.

- Attending a professional meeting for project management professionals to learn about emerging trends and developments.

Once you create your strengths development plan, it is important to execute this plan.

INSTRUCTIONS

1. Complete the Strengths Development Worksheet (**Table 12.4**):
   a. List each of your top five strengths.
   b. Identify your development strategy using the following options as a guide:
      - Reading recently published books or journals.
      - Taking a class to enhance your skill.
      - Finding a mentor.
      - Getting feedback on your skills.
      - Teaching a class on the strength.

- Attending a professional meeting that addresses your strength.

Table 12.4

Strengths Development Worksheet		
Key Strengths	Development Strategy	Frequency or Target Date

c. Identify the target date for your strategy or the frequency with which you will conduct this developmental action, such as monthly, quarterly, or annually.

 Refer to the Resiliency Action Plan Summary Worksheet (**Table 12.6**) at the end of this chapter, capture a strength you want to develop, and write a SMART goal to better develop your strengths. For example: *By November 7 I will complete my development for a major key strength.*

ACTIVITY 5: IDENTIFY OTHER KEY FACTORS THAT HELP YOU FEEL CONFIDENT AND POWERFUL

Identifying and actualizing your strengths are excellent ways to feel confident and powerful, enabling you to assert yourself effectively with others. However, for most people there are other key ingredients that enable a sense of power. By identifying these key ingredients, you will be better prepared for future situations where you need to assert yourself with others. In essence, you will identify your power formula. For example, other key ingredients might include:

- Preparing for tough conversations by envisioning a successful outcome or practicing what you will say.

- Connecting with trusted allies for support prior to facing challenging situations.

- Wearing certain types of clothing that help you feel confident and powerful.

- Getting a good night's rest.

In this activity, you will have an opportunity to reflect on past experiences and use these insights to construct your power formula.

INSTRUCTIONS

1. Complete the Power Formula Worksheet (**Table 12.5**):
   - Identify five examples of situations in your life or work where you felt powerful or confident.
   - For each situation, identify up to three key ingredients that contributed to your feeling of confidence and power.

Table 12.5

Power Formula Worksheet	
Situation	Critical Factors That Helped You Feel Powerful

2. Analyze your responses to the worksheet and identify common themes from the situations you listed. Capture these themes below:
   - Factor #1:
   - Factor #2:
   - Factor #3:
   - Factor #4:
   - Factor #5:

3. Reflect on an upcoming challenge or situation where you need to feel powerful and confident. Identify the perfect outcome you hope for, along with the power ingredients to incorporate in your preparations.

- Situation:

- Successful outcome envisioned:

- Power factors to incorporate:

 Refer to the Resiliency Action Plan Summary Worksheet (**Table 12.6**) at the end of this chapter, capture your most critical power factors, and write a SMART goal to act upon your power formula. For example: *By January 31 I will explore how to incorporate my critical power ingredient into an upcoming challenge I will face.*

RESILIENCY ACTION PLAN SUMMARY WORKSHEET

Refer to the worksheet (**Table 12.6**) to summarize key outcomes and SMART goals from the activities in this chapter.

For each activity associated with this strategy, make sure you have identified a key outcome or SMART goal to help you take action. Capture these commitments in your day planner or calendar to ensure that you complete them.

Table 12.6

☑ Resiliency Action Plan Summary Worksheet	
Activity	**Key Outcome or SMART Goals**
1	
2	
3	
4	
5	

ADDITIONAL RESOURCES

The following resources consist of online videos, apps, and assessment tools that may provide greater depth on key concepts associated with this Resiliency Strategy. We have no control over and do not endorse third-party content, goods, or services.

- Assessing Your Strengths and Weaknesses (Video, 2 minutes). Available at http://bigthink.com/videos/assessing-your-strengths-and-weaknesses.

- Go Put Your Strengths to Work (Video, 3 minutes). Available at http://www.washingtonspeakers.com/wsbtv/view-group. cfm?groupid=406.

- Know Your Strengths, Own Your Strengths (Video, 18 minutes). Available at http://leanin.org/education/know-your-strengths-own-your-strengths-no-one-else-will/.

- StrengthsFinder: Lead with Your Strengths (Online Assessment). Available at https://www.gallupstrengthscenter.com.

THIRTEEN

FRANÇOISE'S STORY: A SECOND CHANCE

BY FRANÇOISE EVENOU

I really see no other solution than to turn inwards and to root out all the rottenness there. I no longer believe that we can change anything in the world until we first change ourselves. And that seems to me the only lesson to be learned.
— ETTY HILLESUM

Five years ago, the book of my life opened a new professional chapter, a fulfilling and fascinating chapter. I became an independent executive coach, senior consultant, and author. I published my first book, *La Rencontre* [The Encounter]. Previously, I had been a corporate executive focused on marketing and communications. Such a significant change does not happen overnight. I went through a deep and long crisis, a period of discovery and transformation.

For fifteen years, I worked in corporate public relations and brand communications. In my late thirties, I was offered a major career opportunity as the new communications director for a global company headquartered in the United States. I felt enthusiastic about my life. I believed I had everything—professional recognition, family love, health, safety, and money. And suddenly, my father died, and I felt a deep void. I began to question all my beliefs.

For the first time in my life, I became aware that we are all finite, and I thought of death. What does living mean if death is at the end of the path? I suddenly felt the urgency to live. I started doing more work, activities, and exercise. I juggled my professional, personal, and family lives. My days became thrilling and fast-paced because I listened only to my desire to be myself, to feel entirely free and alive. For another two years, I assumed I was in full control of my life and being my authentic self. Then one day I broke into tears, exhausted.

That's when I entered the next phase of my crisis. I felt worn out and disoriented. This malaise took the shape of an intense questioning to help me take stock of my life. I scrutinized every single detail of my life, including my marriage, my family, my home, and my work. I looked at what I had accomplished. I asked myself if I was happy. I explored the issue of whether the life I had represented the life I wanted. I questioned if I was successful in my career. I knew I had to explore these questions deeply.

I felt I needed to do some inner work, to become more self-aware. I started a long search to discover my authentic being, my true self. I explored the image I let others see and whether it was the real me. I had spent years building an efficient ego to feel strong and believe in my capabilities. Suddenly, I discovered a gap between my social personality and my deep inner self. I started looking for what was the truest about me. I mustered the courage to look at the idealized image I had of myself. It was a painful phase, but a necessary one if I wanted to discover my authenticity. As C. G. Jung said, "No tree, it is said, can grow to heaven unless its roots reach down to hell."

To support my new introspection and help me find a path toward inner peace, I started reading books at night by writers such as Marcus Aurelius, Carl Gustav Jung, Erich Fromm, and Guy Corneau. This phase was crucial, and I could have made a big step forward if I had developed an awareness of my emotions and the capacity to observe myself with kindness and without judgment. Today, I am convinced that the help of a coach would have been extremely useful at this point, because you need methods, strategies, feedback, and encouragement. I would find this out only years later when I trained to become a coach and learned to develop my emotional intelligence.

Meanwhile, I kept on working for the same company, but my heart wasn't in it anymore. I lacked energy, purpose, and motivation. I felt a growing dissonance between me and the people I worked with, and the strategy and goals of the company. Taking the time for introspection and attempting to find a solution on my own was important, but it went on for too long. I knew I needed help. I made a decision to see a psychiatrist who also had skills as a psychoanalyst.

During this phase, I focused on clarifying my purpose. I took the time to step back and paint a new comprehensive picture of my life, my successes, failures, skills, assets, and values. For the first time in my life, I reflected extensively on my core values. I determined that my values were authenticity, commitment, enthusiasm, freedom, and creativity. By determining my values, I found a road map within by which I could position myself. Using my values as a guide, I put rules of conduct in place to guide my choices and behaviors. To this fundamental question, what's most important to me at this time in the journey, I answered, the search for meaning and self-fulfillment. These insights would be the fuel for my life and the chapter ahead.

Gaining professional achievement was a driving force for me. I always wanted to succeed, but I finally became aware that my current job responsibilities didn't align with how I wanted to advance my career. What motivated me the most was expressing my personal voice, building relationships based on authenticity, and inspiring enthusiasm. That's where I found my energy. I wanted to express my uniqueness, originality, and singularity. I was able to develop a clear vision of my passion for encouraging people to live a true life based on their values, to develop their skills and potential, and to build self-esteem. I discovered my passion for helping others to live and to grow. Coaching appeared to me as a profession that would allow me to feel fulfilled and express my convictions. I wanted to write, to communicate, and share.

At this point, I realized I needed to focus on my self-care, and spirituality appeared to me as essential. Was there something of value that could be the foundation of my life and stand at its center? My psychoanalysis helped me nourish my inner child, my source of wonder and creativity. I was still working for the same company, in the same job, but I started balancing my time in a different way. I started taking time for myself and participating in activities that benefited me. I finally dared to start taking flamenco dancing lessons.

I developed an interest in the great spiritual traditions and ancient teachings. I first turned to the Orient, studying Buddhism, Hinduism, and Sufism. I read, attended seminars, and participated in meditation groups led by well-known masters. Little by little, this led me to discover, deep inside me, the sacred place that was the source of energy and peace. I discovered the divine is within us. I still didn't have the answer to my question, though: What should I do with the rest of my life? Something important was still missing. The answer I had been trying to find for years appeared to me during a three-day stay in a Benedictine monastery. This spiritual experience helped me find the treasure that has occupied an incomparable place in my life for several years now, my faith in Jesus Christ. It took me five years to go through this transformation and come out of the crisis.

I decided to leave my job. I was ready. I needed to move on to something new and vital. I decided to study philosophy and theology. I went back to college, and I felt extremely eager to explore new ways of thinking, to develop new skills, to meet new people, and above all to feed my quest for meaning and spirituality. At age fifty, I decided I wanted to become a coach. I enrolled in a Canadian school based in Paris and broadened my skills by studying systemic approaches. For five years now, I have been an independent coach who specializes in developing leaders.

I do volunteer work with associations that help underprivileged youth find their way in life and develop self-confidence. And a few years ago, I started writing my first book, *La Rencontre* [The Encounter]. I carried this book inside me for so long. It recounts this decisive turning point in my life and my long quest for meaning so I could get onto a path where I would blossom. I published my book, and it represents the beginning of a profoundly gratifying adventure where I meet with others to share and convey. I did not just survive my crisis; I was transformed and thrived. I do believe we can all work our miracles when we become aware of what gives our lives full meaning and plenitude. There are five key lessons that I learned on my journey that I wish to share.

- Having a sense of discernment is crucial if you want to find points of reference and criteria that will help you make the right choice. To make decisions that affect the whole of your existence, you need time and hindsight. When you weather a storm, you may be tempted to abandon the ship altogether, including your job, spouse, and home. You must be vigilant and not make hasty decisions because you are vulnerable and confused.

- A crisis is a time for being and not for doing. It is not surprising that the etymology of the term *crisis* ("krisis" in Greek) would mean breaking point, decision, or judgment. Should I keep going in the same direction? Should I radically change my life? It's important to develop an inner conversation with yourself, connect with your core values, and grant yourself a time out. Even a few days may suffice. You need to find a peaceful and benevolent environment. You can do a retreat, where you will find silence and peace, where all the confused voices in your mind will quiet down to allow you to hear the voice of your conscience.

- It takes courage to make radical changes in our lives. Each time, the task is great. It takes a long time, often many months of emotional investment and reflection. But it's important to face the task, because it leads to a profound inner renewal of energy, purpose, and hope. A midlife crisis can last up to five years on average. It's a crucial passage in one's life, a transition from one phase to another, and a crisis of growth and maturity. It is a period when changes happen that prepare you for the second part of your life. For all those reasons, it represents a unique and fantastic opportunity to rewrite your life script.

- Confronting your limits and admitting you cannot succeed by your strengths alone is a sign of great wisdom. It is important to be both vulnerable and humble. I had to collapse to understand that I had been mistaken and that I needed others, as well as the Other, to bloom.

- Remember to be grateful. I prepared for my meeting with my former manager when I decided to resign my last job, as I needed to remind myself of what the company had allowed me to accomplish. I had made wonderful relationships and shared precious time with others.

Biography

Françoise Evenou is an executive coach and author, living in Paris, married with two children. She loves to help people become themselves. She enjoys traveling, meeting contemporary artists, and reading philosophy and spirituality books. Her book *La Rencontre* has been published by Ed. Nouvelle Cité, March 2015, France, and can be found online at http://www.amazon.fr/ and in French bookstores. You can find more information at www.facebook.com/larencontrelelivre and can contact Françoise via email at francoise.evenou@orange.fr.

FOURTEEN

RESILIENCY STRATEGY: BROADEN COPING SKILLS

Strengthen the skills necessary to reframe the challenge and make intentional choices that lead to growth and thriving, not just surviving.

Coping skills are like a muscle that can be strengthened through consistent awareness, action, and reflection.
— Kevin Nourse

BROADEN COPING SKILLS: ALICIA'S STORY

Alicia made a career change and joined a federal agency nearly ten years ago after a failed attempt to start a graphic design business. The poor economy made it difficult to make a profit. The allure of a regular paycheck, retirement benefits, and tuition reimbursement made her more willing to let go of her entrepreneurial leanings and consider a job in the federal sector. With her skillful attention to detail, graphics expertise, and entrepreneurial mindset, agency customers were always delighted with the quality of her work. Although she was very happy as an individual contributor, Alicia had a number of great ideas for improving the impact of the department, but faced roadblocks with her supervisor, who was resistant to new technology. When the supervisor retired, Alicia applied for the position based on her desire to have more freedom to implement some long-needed improvements in the department. She endured a rigorous panel interview, and after several weeks, she was promoted. Only after she received the notice of her promotion did she realize that the senior publication specialist on her team had also applied for the supervisor role.

Within weeks of her promotion, Alicia noticed strange and confusing behavior by the senior specialist and her manager, the director. While facilitating a brainstorming session on ways to improve efficiency in fulfilling departmental requests, most of the team came up with useful suggestions. However, the senior specialist was completely silent and avoided eye contact. She sat staring at the table and refused to participate, even when Alicia asked the team directly for ideas. On several occasions Alicia noticed the senior specialist walking out of her manager's office. When she asked her manager about these meetings, her manager indicated that the senior specialist was seeking career guidance. Alicia immediately became suspicious about what the senior specialist was saying about her in the mentoring conversations with her manager.

As the weeks wore on in the new role, this individual began to consistently ignore her guidance and requests. Given the service orientation of the publications department, they were expected to remain open from 9 a.m. to 5 p.m. daily. Alicia came in early each day at 7 a.m. and left at 4 p.m. to rush home and pick up her daughter from daycare. One afternoon, she received an email complaint from a manager in another department who had called to order some publications at 4:45 p.m. only to find the department closed. Alicia reached out to one of the junior staff members to find out what happened. Apparently the senior specialist told everyone that Alicia had approved closing the office 15 minutes early. She felt her heart racing and waves of intense anger at what appeared to be insubordination by her employee.

Since she was new to a managerial role, Alicia struggled with how best to handle the situation with her most tenured team member. This employee had a long tenure in the agency, was generally well liked by department heads, and strongly influenced the attitudes of the rest of the team. First she tried to reach out to the senior specialist to find out what might be causing the resistance to Alicia in her supervisory role. In individual meetings, this employee would deny there was an issue and try to change the subject. Alicia was baffled about what was going on. On several attempts to engage her manager for advice on how to handle the situation, her manager canceled the meetings or ended them quickly, claiming other priorities needed attention.

The stress of her work situation was beginning to spill over into Alicia's personal life. She would wake up in the middle of the night ruminating about the events of the day, anticipating worst-case scenarios. She began eating late at night while watching television, and began to gain weight. Alicia became reactive and defensive with the people to whom she was closest. Each morning when she woke up, she still felt tired and groggy. Sunday nights were particularly tough for her, as she worried about the week ahead and slept very little.

Given how uncooperative her senior specialist had been, Alicia decided she would take a stronger stance. She was deeply concerned and angry about how her employee's poor performance was impacting her reputation as well as the department's. While she planned to meet with the employee in a private meeting to address the issues, Alicia's anger and frustration inadvertently exploded at the next staff meeting. The group was exploring one of Alicia's ideas for implementing new technology to improve workflow in the department. Most of the team seemed excited by her proposal. However, the senior publications specialist actively challenged Alicia on her proposal and dismissed it as a stupid idea. Alicia became enraged and confronted the senior publications specialist about the negative attitude and past decision to close the department early without her approval. The meeting quickly dissolved into a highly emotional shouting match between the specialist and Alicia, while the rest of the team silently watched. Her senior specialist marched out of the conference room and slammed the door. After a few moments of awkward silence, Alicia ended the meeting and returned to her office angrier than ever, determined to find a way to fire her employee.

Ultimately, the senior specialist filed a harassment complaint against Alicia, deepening her frustration and her sense of hopelessness about the situation. She found out about the complaint from her manager in one of their biweekly meetings. The tone of the conversation led Alicia to believe that her manager was not interested in her point of view on how the issues had unfolded. Alicia was surprised, since she believed she had established a supportive relationship with her manager. Alicia felt herself grow defensive and angry, as she blamed the senior specialist for creating this issue. The meeting quickly ended with her manager explaining that she would take over day-to-day management of the team until the investigation was complete. In her mind, Alicia began to panic, as she concluded that she had lost any support she had from her manager.

In the weeks after the meeting with her manager, Alicia struggled with feelings of betrayal, anger, and embarrassment. She was not coping well with the situation. Because of her embarrassment, she felt isolated and avoided her closest friends, who did not understand why Alicia had become so distant. She often ruminated about how this whole situation happened and what it meant for her career, especially at night when she tried to sleep. She often felt her heart racing with panic at the thought of losing her job and being unable to pay her mortgage. Alicia became impatient with her daughter and snapped at her at random for making noise. Also, Alicia continued to eat junk food while watching television at night, despite not being hungry.

While her manager conducted the weekly team meetings after the blow-up in the staff meeting, Alicia finally uncovered information that filled in the missing parts of the puzzle. Alicia could feel the tension with the senior specialist and remained quiet without contributing. Much to Alicia's surprise, at one point in the meeting her manager announced that the senior specialist would take over a high-visibility project that Alicia had been managing. Upon announcing this in the meeting, her boss smiled at the senior specialist. Alicia noticed everyone looking at her to gauge her reaction. It took every ounce of energy for Alicia to avoid exploding at her boss, but she said nothing.

After the meeting, Alicia returned to her office and thought about all that had happened. She reached out to a colleague in another department, who revealed some surprising information. Apparently, rumors in the agency suggested that the director had promised the supervisor position to the senior specialist. When Alicia applied for the position, the panel of interviewers really liked her qualifications and recommended that she receive the promotion. While the department director wanted to promote the senior publication specialist, the agency deputy administrator was the decision maker who chose Alicia. These rumors made it painfully apparent to Alicia that she had completely ignored the relationship between her senior specialist and her manager, which resulted in her career being sabotaged. She wondered how she could have been so naïve about the relationship between them and missed some obvious clues. For days afterward, Alicia emotionally beat herself up for making so many mistakes in how she handled this situation.

DERAILMENT TRIGGERS

Alicia's story contains some critical derailment triggers that likely contributed to the painful experience she endured:

1. **Ignoring the signs of sabotage.**

   Most people like to believe that coworkers and bosses are trustworthy and transparent, yet the reality is that sabotage happens and can easily derail careers. By ignoring the signs of collusion between her subordinate and her boss, Alicia was set up to fail in her role.

2. **Unchecked emotional reactions.**

   Unchecked emotional reactions to others often contribute to a deepening of conflict in a self-fulfilling cycle of reaction, blaming, defensiveness, and damaged trust.

3. **Dysfunctional emotions-based coping.**

   Getting stuck in one's emotions can also block rational thinking, which is essential to identifying options for navigating career adversity. Unproductive coping with uncomfortable emotions can also be manifest in terms of seeking unhealthy ways to resolve one's feelings, such as overeating, drinking, or other addictions.

4. **Unwilling to ask for help.**

   Asking for help is a very useful problem-centered strategy to cope with adversity. People who do not know how to ask for help or are fearful of doing so often delay or block their ability to recover and thrive.

Each of the derailment triggers in Alicia's story can either be avoided or minimized through proactive reflection and action.

DERAILMENT TRIGGER QUESTIONS

In light of the derailment triggers identified in Alicia's story, there are several useful questions to reflect on as a way to prevent adversity in your career:

- How would I recognize sabotage of my career by others, and what would I do if this happened?

- To what extent am I able to manage my emotions and not let them control me?

- How effective am I at using problem-centered approaches in coping with tough times?

- Am I able to ask for help when faced with career adversity?

- What do I say to myself when I make a mistake? To what extent do I use positive self-talk in the process of coping with tough times?

By asking yourself these questions in advance, you can anticipate potential career challenges, your options for coping with them, and therefore ensure you maintain your resiliency.

DEFINING 'BROADEN COPING SKILLS'

Broadening your coping skills involves strengthening the skills necessary to reframe your challenge and making choices that lead to growth and thriving, not just surviving. One of the most critical factors enabling resilient people to grow from tough times is the way they make sense of and cope with adverse situations. If you view the career adversity you face as a threat, you will most likely use fight-or-flight behavior and become either overly aggressive or passive in facing tough situations. If you frame tough times as a challenge, you will likely move toward your challenge, cope more powerfully, and therefore achieve better outcomes.

A more functional way to cope with adversity involves both emotions and problem-based responses. Ideally, the first challenge is to recognize and manage our emotional reactions to adversity, taking care to avoid getting trapped in them. Resilient people recognize that when they face adversity, their initial reactions on how to respond may not be the most effective. Therefore, important coping strategies for managing your emotions include asking for emotional support from trusted supporters and getting perspective on your challenges. One way to get perspective is to disengage temporarily from the battle through activities such as exercise or getting involved in some of your passions and interests. By giving yourself permission to disengage temporarily using healthy and functional activities, you will be better equipped to think clearly about the way forward.

With your emotions in check, you are then ready to tackle the source of the career adversity in front of you through problem-based coping strategies. These strategies involve using your cognitive skills and include reframing, problem-solving, planning, and taking action. Reframing situations allows you to shift your perspective to look at what happened through different lenses. For example, some people who lose their jobs due to organizational downsizing can reframe the loss as an opportunity to explore new career options they were hesitant to consider in the past. Problem-solving, either alone or with others, can give you insights on how to correct mistakes you might have made in the past and explore options for the future. Planning involves identifying your goals and creating an action plan with milestones to move forward. Some people also include scenario planning as part of this strategy, where they identify options for the future, explore the best and worst outcomes, and upgrade their plans based on insights they gain. Finally, taking action based on the plans you created is an excellent way to begin the journey to rebuilding your resiliency.

A growth mindset is demonstrated in the way people talk to themselves. Those who can choose a growth mindset recognize they can adapt and grow in the face of adversity. Self-talk for people embracing a growth mindset is empowering and self-affirming. Those with fixed mindsets resist growth and assume that their skills and abilities are fixed and unchangeable. Both of these mindsets can contribute to a self-fulfilling prophecy. If you believe you can grow and learn from adversity, chances are very good that this will happen.

The way you talk to yourself throughout the process of coping with tough times is vital. Being positive enables you to embrace a growth mindset. Growth-oriented people use positive, nonjudgmental language when they experience challenges. Examples include:

- *I know I will grow from this challenge.*

- *What are my options?*

- *Is there another way I can view this situation?*

- *I believe in my ability to grow from this experience.*

- *What did I learn from this experience?*

- *What would I do differently as a result of this challenge?*

Examples of fixed-mindset people and the self-talk they use:

- *You screwed that up again.*

- *Why bother?*

- *What's wrong with me?*

- *How could I be so stupid?*

- *I'll never be as successful as X!*

Increasing the experience of positive emotions and reducing the frequency of negative emotions has been shown to contribute to the ability of people to maintain their sense of resiliency. Positive emotions can range from joy or pride to awe and love. Negative emotions, such as anger, frustration, and contempt have a tendency to inhibit resiliency. By eliminating the sources of negative emotions in your life and enhancing the conditions that trigger positive emotions, you can better prepare yourself for adversity and ensure resilient outcomes. If you experience the right ratio of positive to negative emotions, you can help broaden your perspective so that you are more equipped to anticipate challenges and prepare for them long before they become a crisis. Broadening and strengthening your coping skills can help you lessen the emotional depths you experience during tough times as well as speed up the pace of rebounding from adversity.

BROADEN COPING SKILLS ACTION STEPS

There are five action steps within *Broaden Coping Skills* that can be taken to help you strengthen the skills necessary to reframe the challenge and make intentional choices that lead to growth and thriving, not just surviving:

1. Embrace a growth mindset in the way you talk to yourself about your challenges.

2. Use scenario planning to envision the best and worst cases.

3. Identify effective ways to get perspective on your challenges.

4. Identify aspects of challenges that you can and cannot control.

5. Increase the frequency of positive emotions and decrease the frequency of negative emotions.

You can use the Resiliency Action Plan to help broaden your coping skills. By broadening your coping skills, you will be able to avoid getting trapped in the emotions that are triggered by adversity and more powerfully cope with your challenges. When people actively manage their challenges, they are more likely to achieve resilient outcomes and thrive.

Consider the powerful example of Malala Yousafzai. She is a young Pakistani girl who was shot point-blank by Taliban gunmen in 2012 and survived to speak to the United Nations a year later about her dream for improving conditions for girls around the world. Malala and her father received death threats because of their outspoken views about education for girls in a country where the Taliban was increasingly hostile toward basic freedoms for women. Her injuries were nearly fatal, with a bullet piercing her head and neck.

Despite her injuries, Malala avoided getting trapped by her emotions in the ways she coped. Rather than focus on her survival and physical well-being, she was more worried about how to reunite with her family, since she was being treated in the United Kingdom. Within days of the shooting, she explained:

> I always think about solutions to problems, so I thought maybe I could go down to the reception of the hospital and ask for a phone to call my mother and father. But my brain was telling me, *You don't have the money to pay for the call, nor do you know the country code.* Then I thought, *I need to get out and start working to earn money so I can buy a phone and call my father so we can all be together again.*

Malala also drew upon two other strategies to cope with her potentially debilitating injuries. She recalled how much reading helped her navigate the road to recovery. In particular, she read *The Wonderful Wizard of Oz*, explaining "I loved reading about Dorothy and how even though she was trying to get back home she stopped and helped those in need ... She had to overcome a lot of obstacles to get where she was going, and I thought if you want to achieve a goal, there will be hurdles in your way, but you must continue." Malala also described how she was able to reframe a tragedy into a powerful vision for herself. She explained, "I know God stopped me from going to the grave. It feels like this life is a second life ... I was spared for a reason—to use my life for helping people."

Although she had every reason to succumb to the physical pain associated with her injuries or become consumed with anger toward her shooters, Malala continues to resiliently thrive in her quest to improve the plight of children. Her resiliency at such an early age and capacity to grow from adversity no doubt contributed to her being selected in October 2014 as the winner of the Nobel Peace Prize.

BROADEN COPING SKILLS:
ALICIA'S RESILIENCY ACTION PLAN

Alicia realized that she needed to cope more effectively with her work situation to move forward. First, she recognized that she was too close to the situation to have a clear sense of how to move forward. At the suggestion of a good friend, she made arrangements to visit a spa in a nearby city for a weekend to relax, eat healthy, and reflect on all that had happened in her job. When she first arrived at the spa, she was unable to let go and relax. Eventually she began to feel calmer after swimming in the heated pool, going for a long walk, and writing in her journal.

One of the books she read included stories about women who faced tremendous challenges in their careers and thrived. Alicia decided that whatever the outcome of her work situation, she was committed to growing from this painful experience and would not allow it to define her career. As a result, she began to notice and change the negative self-talk that kept her stuck in a pattern of anger, frustration, denial, and defensiveness. Rather than accept these negative messages, she began to challenge those beliefs and replace them with more empowering self-talk messages that helped her feel better and take action.

In the weeks after her mini-retreat, Alicia began to dramatically shift her mindset toward all that had happened as well as consider new options for her future. One of the most significant shifts happened when she began to reframe the painful work situation from an embarrassing and painful chapter to a potential career opportunity. Recalling her long-dormant interest in becoming an entrepreneur, Alicia began to envision what it might look like to try again to launch her own graphics business. She also made a commitment to herself to consciously manage her life to increase the frequency of positive emotions and eliminate situations that triggered negative emotions for her.

While the thought of starting a business excited her and seemed like a much better fit for her personality, she still felt anxiety at leaving her job and a steady paycheck. However, Alicia did not let the emotions block her from moving forward. When this fear emerged, she would engage some trusted supporters to talk of her fears. By doing so, she was then able to continue working on a business plan to better define her dream and address the issues that might block her success. As part of her business plan, she explored best and worst-case scenarios for the first year of her business. This planning process allowed her to uncover potential roadblocks and explore potential options to ensure her success.

Because Alicia realized that she had options beyond her current role, her attitude at work shifted substantially. Human resources finished the investigation and concluded there was no evidence of harassment. Because this was the first time it had happened, her manager gave her a verbal warning. Alicia returned to her role as supervisor. Rather than react defensively when her boss met privately with the senior specialist on her team, Alicia reminded herself that she had no control over the interactions between them. Rather, she focused on her emerging vision for becoming an entrepreneur and the progress she was making in unfolding this dream. The relationship between her and her boss improved notably, and there was less tension with her senior specialist. Rather than getting bogged down in strong emotions, Alicia was able to evoke positive emotions by calling forth images in her mind of being an entrepreneur and having freedom to pursue her passions. She slept better at night, since the fear and worry about her future was gone. Because she had decided to leave the agency and relaunch her business, Alicia decided to let go of her sense of betrayal triggered by the sabotage by her boss and senior employee.

After several months of planning and preparing to launch her business, Alicia finally had a conversation with her manager about her plans to leave the agency. Her boss was genuinely surprised when Alicia announced she wanted to leave her role and launch her own business, but eventually agreed it would be a great opportunity for her. Much to Alicia's surprise, her boss even suggested that they would consider engaging Alicia as a consultant to design the graphics for departmental projects. Alicia left the conversation realizing how far she had come from the painful place she was in and excited about the future she had created for herself.

BROADEN COPING SKILLS: RESILIENCY ACTION PLAN ACTIVITIES

The purpose of this strategy is to help you strengthen the skills necessary to reframe the challenge and make choices that lead to growth and thriving, not just surviving. There are five action steps that you can take to help broaden your coping skills:

1. Embrace a growth mindset in the way you talk to yourself about your challenges.

2. Use scenario planning to envision the best and worst cases.

3. Identify effective ways to get perspective on your challenges.

4. Identify aspects of a challenge that you can and cannot control.

5. Increase the frequency of positive emotions and decrease the frequency of negative emotions.

The following five activities will help you take action to broaden your coping strategies.

ACTIVITY 1: EMBRACE A GROWTH MINDSET IN THE WAY YOU TALK TO YOURSELF ABOUT YOUR CHALLENGES

This activity will help you make conscious choices on what you want to say to yourself when facing a tough challenge. The self-talk you use can make a huge difference in how you respond to challenges, take action, and achieve outcomes.

INSTRUCTIONS

1. Reflect on a current challenge you are facing and pay attention to what you say to yourself about the challenge.

2. While referring to the worksheet (**Table 14.1**), capture any negative self-talk messages:

    a. Negative self-talk message you unconsciously say to yourself.

    b. Events or conditions that trigger this negative message. For example, perhaps there are certain people or situations that cause you to send negative self-talk messages to yourself. Alternatively, maybe it's a specific time of day or instances when you do not get enough sleep.

    c. Identify evidence that refutes this negative message. For example, if your negative self-talk message is "No other employer would hire me," you might capture examples such as "A headhunter called last week and was interested in my background" or "Five job postings appeared on LinkedIn last week for people with my skills."

    d. Alternative growth-oriented self-talk message. Reword your negative self-talk message to become more empowering and growth-oriented. For example, "No other employer would hire me" could be reworded as "I have highly desirable skills and could choose to explore other career options."

Table 14.1

Self-Talk Assessment Worksheet			
Negative Self-Talk Message	Trigger	Evidence That Contradicts	Alternative Growth-Oriented Message

 Refer to the Resiliency Action Plan Summary Worksheet (**Table 14.6**) at the end of this chapter and identify a SMART goal associated with actions you could take to incorporate your new growth-oriented messages into your mindset. For example, *Establish a practice or ritual every morning and read your alternative growth-oriented messages aloud.*

ACTIVITY 2: USE SCENARIO PLANNING TO ENVISION THE BEST AND WORST CASES

This activity will help you articulate the best and worst-case scenarios as a means of prompting yourself to use problem-centered coping to respond to your challenge. Scenario planning is often used by organizations during a strategic planning process to surface and test assumptions about the future. When people face career adversity, they may experience an ambiguous sense of anxiety that keeps them stuck because they continually think about it. By articulating these scenarios on paper, it allows you to use your thinking brain to explore ways to ensure the best case happens and the worst case is avoided.

INSTRUCTIONS

1. Reflect on a current challenge you are facing. Notice the feelings, messages, and internal beliefs you are experiencing.

2. Identify the best-case scenario, as if everything works out perfectly. For example, assume your organization is about to launch a downsizing initiative and reduce the size of its workforce. Perhaps the best-case scenario is that you get to hold on to your job and receive a promotion because of additional responsibilities you are asked to take on. With the additional money you are paid, you then take a dream vacation or invest the money in your retirement. Write this scenario in the past tense, as if it already happened, and pay attention to your feelings and emotions as you write it. Reflect on this scenario and capture ideas for the following questions:

    a. What are some of the assumptions implicit in this scenario (e.g., my skills are needed by my organization)?

    b.   What could I do to help this scenario unfold?

    c.   Who could help me unfold this scenario?

3. Explore the worst-case scenario based on catastrophic outcomes. Using the same example, maybe your worst-case scenario is that you lose your job and do not receive any severance compensation. As a result, you cannot pay your mortgage and lose your home. Write this scenario in the past tense and pay attention to your emotions. Reflect on the scenario with the following questions:

    a.   What assumptions did I make in this scenario (e.g., I lose my job but am not allowed to apply for other jobs, or I am not perceived as effective in my job)?

    b.   What data exists to support or refute each of your assumptions?

    c.   How likely is this worst-case scenario?

    d.   If this scenario did occur, what could be some of the unexpected positive outcomes (e.g., leave a job or company you never really enjoyed)?

    e.   What actions could you take to prevent this worst-case scenario?

    f.   Who would you turn to if the worst-case scenario happened?

 Refer to the Resiliency Action Plan Summary Worksheet (**Table 14.6**) at the end of this chapter and capture a few words that describe your worst-case scenario along with a SMART goal to help you reflect on the outcomes of tough challenges you faced and insights you gained on how you coped with them.

ACTIVITY 3: IDENTIFY EFFECTIVE WAYS TO GET PERSPECTIVE ON YOUR CHALLENGES

Before most people are able to take action to address career adversity, they have to get perspective on their issues by disconnecting from strong emotions and engaging their thinking brains. Gaining perspective can take a variety of forms, not all of which are healthy or productive. This is particularly true when people avoid facing their challenges indefinitely, which can result in poor outcomes. A glass of wine to relax after a tough meeting can be incredibly effective, but taken to an extreme, it can significantly diminish your effectiveness and lead to an addiction. In this activity, you will identify various types of actions you can take to get perspective on tough challenges you face from a psychological, spiritual, or physical perspective.

INSTRUCTIONS

1. Reflect on a past challenge you faced in your life or career. Capture five strategies you used to gain perspective on your challenge below (e.g., went to the gym, ate comfort food, got a good night's sleep, etc.):
   a. Strategy 1:
   b. Strategy 2:
   c. Strategy 3:
   d. Strategy 4:
   e. Strategy 5:

2. Review the list from step 1 and identify those strategies that were the most healthy and effective in helping you gain perspective that you might use again in the future.

3. Review the list of potential strategies below and check all those you might add to your list of options to use when you face future career adversities:
   a. Prayer or meditation.
   b. Yoga.
   c. Swimming.
   d. Running.
   e. A good night's sleep.

f.   Time with friends.

g.   Reading books on how well-known personalities faced tough times.

h.   Watching movies about how well-known personalities faced tough times.

i.   Reading spiritual books.

j.   Listening to music.

k.   Creating art.

l.   Working in the garden.

m.   Building something.

n.   Journal writing.

o.   Seeking help from a coach, therapist, counselor, or minister.

p.   Having a good cry.

q.   Getting a massage.

r.   Soaking in a hot bath.

  Refer to the Resiliency Action Plan Summary Worksheet (**Table 14.6**) at the end of this chapter and capture two new coping strategies you want to use in the future. Identify a SMART goal associated with actions you could take to be ready to use those new strategies the next time you face a tough situation. For example, *By November 23, I will identify a skilled and affordable massage therapist I can engage when I face a really tough work situation.*

ACTIVITY 4: IDENTIFY ASPECTS OF CHALLENGES THAT YOU CAN AND CANNOT CONTROL

This activity will help you clarify where you can and cannot control a challenging situation you face. Many times, when people face a challenge but do not perceive they can control or influence the outcome, they tend to give up. By focusing on aspects of a situation you can control, you are more likely to be optimistic that your actions can lead to positive outcomes. In this activity, you will first be asked to reflect on past challenges you faced where you did not initially believe you could have any impact. Secondly, you will then be asked to reflect on an upcoming challenge and identify factors you could control or influence.

INSTRUCTIONS

1. Reflect on past challenges in your life and work that you initially perceived as overwhelming and identify three examples in the Control & Influence Assessment worksheet (**Table 14.2**). For each example, capture the following:

   a. A description of the situation.

   b. Initial reaction to the challenge.

   c. Situational factors you were able to directly control.

   d. Situational factors you were able to influence.

   e. Situational factors beyond your control or influence.

   f. Outcome of your efforts to respond to the situation or challenge.

   g. Lessons you learned, especially about your initial reaction and strategies for coping with the situation or challenge.

2. Based on this analysis, summarize your insights about yourself and the way you respond to and cope with challenging circumstances on notepaper or in a personal journal.

3. Consider a current or potential challenge you are facing in your career. Based on the analysis of your past experiences:

   a. How do you want to view this situation?

   b. What can you control or influence about this situation?

   c. What is beyond your control or influence in this situation?

   d. What coping strategies do you want to use based on what worked well in the past?

Table 14.2

Control and Influence Assessment Worksheet			
	Example 1	**Example 2**	**Example 3**
Situation or Challenge			
Your Initial Reaction			
Factors You Could Control			
Factors You Could Influence			
Factors Beyond Your Control			
Outcome			
Lessons Learned			

e.   What coping strategies do you want to avoid based on what did not work so well in the past?

 Refer to the Resiliency Action Plan Summary Worksheet (**Table 14.6**) at the end of this chapter and capture one example of a factor you can personally control. Also, identify a SMART goal to remind yourself to perform this activity on a periodic basis, such as monthly or quarterly, to handle challenges that feel overwhelming and aspects you can and cannot control.

ACTIVITY 5: INCREASE THE FREQUENCY OF POSITIVE EMOTIONS AND DECREASE THE FREQUENCY OF NEGATIVE EMOTIONS

This activity is designed to help you increase the frequency of positive emotions and decrease the frequency of negative emotions. By doing so, you can augment your resiliency by building resources you can draw upon the next time you are faced with tough times.

INSTRUCTIONS

1. Reflect on positive situations in both your work and personal life that occurred in the past year and capture five examples in the worksheet below (**Table 14.3**) or in your personal journal:

   a. Capture the situation when you experienced the positive emotions.

   b. Identify situational factors that were present, such as the physical location, time of day, people you were with, and your behavior or actions.

   c. Close your eyes and visualize yourself in the experience. Capture the emotions you are experiencing as you reflect on the situation.

Table 14.3

Positive Emotions Inventory Worksheet		
Situation	Situational Factors	Positive Emotions Experienced

2. Identify five situations that trigger negative emotions in your work and personal life (**Table 14.4**):

Table 14.4

Negative Emotions Inventory Worksheet		
Situation	Situational Factors	Negative Emotions Experienced

3. Analyze both worksheets and identify one positive emotion you want to experience more frequently and one negative emotion you want to decrease or eliminate. Capture them in the worksheet (**Table 14.5**) and brainstorm actions you can take. For example, let's say you want to experience more joy. Perhaps you could:

Table 14.5

Positive and Negative Emotion Action Plan Worksheet		
Targeted Emotion	Action Steps To: Increase Positive Emotions Decrease Negative Emotions	Target Date
Positive Emotions		
Negative Emotions		

- Visit a local art gallery and observe beautiful art.
- Purchase fresh flowers once a week and keep them by your bed.
- Go for a walk in a local park to spend more time in nature.
- Create a gratitude list and update it daily.

To reduce your experience of a negative emotion such as stress, consider actions such as:

- Writing your thoughts and feelings in a journal.
- Taking a hot bath before bed.
- Reading a book or taking a class on negotiations to learn how to better negotiate what you want in your job.
- Ending a relationship with a friend that is consistently creating stress and anxiety.
- Committing to leave a job that is toxic for you.

 Refer to the Resiliency Action Plan Summary Worksheet (**Table 14.6**) at the end of this chapter and capture one positive emotion you want to experience more frequently and one negative emotion you want to eliminate. Consider identifying a SMART goal to set your intentions of positive emotions you want to experience more frequently. For example, *I will schedule*

a long walk in a nearby park every Saturday morning with my spouse.

RESILIENCY ACTION PLAN SUMMARY WORKSHEET

Refer to the worksheet (**Table 14.6**) to summarize key outcomes and SMART goals from the activities in this chapter.

For each activity associated with this strategy, make sure you have identified a key outcome or SMART goal to help you take action. Capture these commitments in your day planner or calendar to ensure you complete them.

Table 14.6

✅	Resiliency Action Plan Summary Worksheet
Activity	**Key Outcome or SMART Goals**
1	
2	
3	
4	
5	

ADDITIONAL RESOURCES

The following resources consist of online videos, apps, and assessment tools that may provide greater depth on key concepts associated with this Resiliency Strategy. We have no control over and do not endorse third-party content, goods, or services.

- Barbara Fredrickson: The Positivity Ratio (Video, 9 minutes). Available at https://www.youtube.com/watch?v=_hFzxfQpLjM.

- Carol Dweck: The power of believing that you can improve (Video, 10 minutes). Available at https://www.ted.com/talks/carol_dweck_the_power_of_believing_that_you_can_improve

- Headspace (App). Meditation and mindfulness app to help reduce your stress and anxiety. Available at https://www.headspace.com.

- Kellie Nightlinger: Develop positive coping skills when facing adversity (Video, 3 minutes). Available at https://youtu.be/kDbwVV3hXgE.

- Relax Melodies (App). Soothing sounds to help you relax and sleep. Available at http://www.ipnossoft.com

FIFTEEN

A CALL TO ACTION

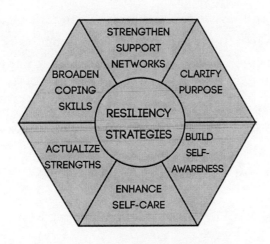

Look upon yesterday with openness and ask "What did I learn?" Look upon today with curiosity and ask "How can I grow?" Look upon tomorrow with anticipation and say "I will thrive."
— LYNN SCHMIDT

NEXT STEPS

You have now come to the last chapter of the book. So, what is the next step? The primary purpose of this book is to provide women with strategies and tools to help them build their resiliency. By using these strategies, women will become more empowered to self-coach and thrive, not just survive work-related challenges.

The second purpose is to provide people developers, including professional coaches, human resource professionals, and managers, with an understanding of what challenges women face at work. With this understanding and supporting strategies, those who coach and mentor women will be better equipped to coach women on building resiliency.

A third purpose of the book is to provide organizational leaders with insights on the issues that women encounter at work and suggestions for how they can use the strategies to help women become more resilient. In this book, the term *organizational* is defined as any organization where women work, such as schools, nonprofit organizations, and for-profit businesses. It also refers to organizations that support the development of people developers and women, such as colleges and universities.

The fourth purpose is to educate men about the experiences that women face in the workforce. Men play an important role in supporting the success of women at work. Another reason for men to read the book is that many of the resiliency strategies can apply to men, too. Men have indicated that by using these strategies, they can build their resiliency as well.

Depending on which audience you belong to, the next steps will be different. This chapter has four sections:

- A call to action for women

- A call to action for people developers

- A call to action for organizational leaders

- A call to action for men

While each section provides specific suggestions for next steps, the suggestions are not all-inclusive. But they can help you generate additional ideas that are a good fit for you or your organization.

A CALL TO ACTION FOR WOMEN

Women need to take action to build their own resiliency and support other women. Supporting other women as they build their resiliency and strengthen their networks is critically important. This call to action for women includes two sections: (1) your Resiliency Action Plan, and (2) women supporting women.

YOUR RESILIENCY ACTION PLAN

After taking the assessment and reviewing the strategy chapters, you should be aware of the changes you need to make to become more resilient. The call to action is for you to create your Resiliency Action Plan and implement it. All of the tools and resources needed to do so have been provided. Use the following four steps outlined in chapter 2 to help create and implement your plan. Remember, you should build your plan proactively before you are in a challenging work situation.

1. Complete the self-assessment that will allow you to identify the Resiliency Strategies you most need to focus on right now.

2. Create your Resiliency Action Plan to guide your exploration of the activities associated with each Resiliency Strategy.

3. Implement the specific Resiliency Strategies you have selected, and refer to the Resiliency Action Plan Summary Worksheet at the end of each chapter.

4. Use self-coaching as a way of helping you take action with your Resiliency Action Plan and goals.

Be sure to celebrate your successes. Treat yourself to something you enjoy when goals are accomplished and your resiliency is increasing. Review your plan regularly and reassess to see if there are other strategies you should focus on to build your resiliency. Life changes, and you may find that the original strategies on your plan are no longer the priorities.

WOMEN SUPPORTING WOMEN

The women interviewed for this book frequently commented that women were not supporting other women in the workplace. Rather than helping each other, work was depicted as a culture of every woman for herself, creating a competitive environment. Sometimes women were described as the saboteurs of other women; other times they were described as acting like ostriches, with their heads in the sand, ignoring workplace realities. There is a perception that the only way women will be able to make changes to work-related gender issues, policies, and practices is if they join together. That is how change has happened for women over the centuries. It is how women were able to get to vote, and it was how they changed employment laws.

Women need to acknowledge the common issues that they all face and support one another in the search for career satisfaction. Not only does supporting other women and their efforts to achieve career satisfaction help the recipient of this support, it also contributes to your own resiliency-building efforts. There are many actions women can take to demonstrate support that do not require extensive efforts. Below is a short list to help you begin to generate ideas.

- Inform young women about the challenges they will encounter at work and how they can build resiliency. This may mean talking with your daughter about the topic. It may mean becoming involved in college associations, or serving as a mentor in a volunteer organization for young women and girls. During the interviews conducted for this book, many women commented that they wished they had learned about work-related challenges in college instead of having to navigate them in the workplace.

- Join a women's professional organization. You can select one specific to the profession you are in or one focused on working women in general. Some probably meet in-person in the city you live in, which is a good way to connect and build a local network. Others meet virtually, which allows for expanding your network more easily. Once you join, get involved. If you are uncomfortable networking with strangers, consider reaching out to the program or membership director in the organization, who can help introduce you to others. Support your colleagues in their professional activities.

- Get involved with your organization's women's resource group. Many companies have internal women's resource groups, and the members are women who work for the company. Attend the educational sessions that are offered and get to know the women in your organization. Offer support when women encounter challenges, and when you hear of issues and concerns.

- Become a mentor. There are many ways to serve as a mentor to another woman. You can be a peer mentor by mentoring a friend or colleague. You can mentor someone newer to your profession or organization. You can mentor someone outside your profession or organization. Sometimes all a woman needs is another woman to listen to her concerns or issues and provide guidance or advice. And other times it can be helpful to have someone provide support as you make a career move or seek a promotion.

- Buy from women-owned businesses. There are many products and services offered by woman-owned businesses. Do your research and find one that provides what you need.

- Support other women's career endeavors. You can demonstrate support in many simple ways. If a woman you know is launching a new business, product, or service, tell your friends and family. Share her information on Facebook. Like her post on LinkedIn. Sign up for her website newsletter. Buy her product. Congratulate her. Connect her to others who may be interested. Most of these actions only take a few minutes of your time, but the woman will consider your support invaluable.

- Simply be present. Many women encounter difficult times related to their careers. These experiences can be embarrassing, painful, and devastating. Sometimes women are not comfortable sharing these experiences. Recognize the signs, ask how you can help, and listen. That may be all she needs to know someone understands and cares.

Women supporting women will have a significant impact on building resiliency. It touches each of the six strategies in a multitude of ways and is directly related to building networks. You are now aware. Make a commitment today to support other women.

A CALL TO ACTION FOR THOSE IN A PEOPLE DEVELOPER ROLE

Those in a people developer role, including professional coaches, human resource professionals, and managers, play an important role in helping women build their resiliency. The call to action for those in a people developer role is (1) to develop knowledge about the work-related challenges women face, which are different from what men encounter, and (2) develop skills to effectively coach and mentor women facing difficult work-related challenges, as it requires a different skill set. Many of the women who participated in the research conducted for this book indicated that a coach played a significant role in helping them strengthen their resiliency and thrive in the face of work-related challenges. These coaches were knowledgeable about the issues women faced in the workplace and had developed skill in coaching and mentoring.

DEVELOP KNOWLEDGE ABOUT THE WORK-RELATED CHALLENGES WOMEN FACE

Reading articles and books, as well as talking with women about their experiences, are all great ways to develop knowledge about the work-related issues women face. Even if you are a female coach or mentor, you will find it helpful to broaden your knowledge base.

- This book contains a great deal of information on the issues women face in the workplace. Chapters 1 and 2 provide research-related examples. The women's stories, those written by women and those within each strategy chapter (chapters 3–14), give significant insights into the challenges women encounter.

- The Notes section of this book supplies additional resources to increase your knowledge.

- Searching the Internet will provide articles, books, and other resources.

- If you are going to be coaching or mentoring women, find women to talk with that you are not coaching or mentoring who will share their work challenges with you. This will provide insights that will be helpful.

The role of a people developer in helping women thrive, not just survive, work-related challenges is important. When people developers understand the issues women face at work, they are better able to help them achieve satisfaction. Determine what knowledge you need and take action.

DEVELOP SKILLS TO EFFECTIVELY COACH AND MENTOR WOMEN FACING DIFFICULT WORK-RELATED CHALLENGES

There are many coaching competency models that identify the skills required to effectively coach or mentor. For this book, several coaches were interviewed, and hundreds were invited to take a follow-up survey to determine the critical competencies needed to coach women experiencing workplace challenges. The International Coach Federation (ICF) competency model, which has eleven competencies used to assess coaches, was used as the baseline. Coaches were asked to identify which of the eleven ICF competencies were most critical when coaching a woman to build resiliency when facing work-related challenges. While the ICF competencies were developed specific to the role of coaching, they can be applied to mentoring as well.

Competencies focused on establishing the coaching relationship and using effective communication methods are important to every coaching engagement. They are foundational skills. The following five competencies are the most critical when coaching women experiencing a career challenge. Those who coach must demonstrate a high level of skill in these five competencies to help women being coached thrive and transform.

1. Establish trust and intimacy with women being coached. The ability for the coach to create a safe and supportive environment based on mutual trust is important, especially in situations where women did not request coaching. The coach should demonstrate honesty and integrity, and keep promises. Coaches who demonstrate an empathetic understanding of the challenges women face in the workplace are often able to build a deep sense of trust with women clients and thereby achieve greater results.

2. Be present as a coach, using a style that is open, flexible, and confident. Given the nature of challenging work situations, coaches have to be comfortable working with strong emotions without being overpowered. Coaches need to be able to help their clients shift perspective and see new possibilities for action.

3. Use multiple sources of data to create awareness. This information may come from the women being coached, interviews with managers, peers, and direct reports, as well as assessments. The coach needs to create awareness in a very direct way to diffuse any denial and to help women recognize the choices they have to grow from adversity. It is important to enable women to see how to maximize strengths and develop critical competencies to take action. Many of the strategies offered in this book were identified by coaches who work with women based on the awareness-building activities they suggested for their clients. By building a strong level of awareness, women receiving coaching experience deeper learning from the coaching engagement and achieve more powerful outcomes.

4. Co-create actions with the women being coached that will lead to results. The actions that coaches co-create with women are critical

to them developing the ability for resiliency. Leveraging the activities in this book, coaches need to focus the women on agreed-upon coaching goals and promote experimentation and self-discovery that requires the application of what has been learned. It is important to challenge assumptions and celebrate successes.

5. Manage the progress and accountability of the women being coached. Focus the attention of the women on the Resiliency Action Plan provided in this book, ensuring that they take action. Because of the visibility of the coaching engagement with key stakeholders, demonstrating progress and maintaining accountability is essential both for the coaches and the women being coached. Be comfortable confronting the women if they do not take the agreed-upon actions. Use the Resiliency Action Plan to manage accountability.

Women can achieve transformative outcomes personally and professionally when the six resiliency strategies are combined with a coach's skill in using the preceding competencies. It is important for coaches to become familiar with the six resiliency strategies that are the focus of this book and to be able to coach women using the tools and techniques provided.

When the six strategies are used in combination with the five competencies, the women being coached experience improved self-development and satisfaction that transcends their professional lives into personal domains. Women gain greater awareness of their value and talents, leading to enhanced confidence, presence, and the ability to be an advocate for themselves. This causes women to set stronger boundaries with their professional duties, allowing them to achieve a more satisfying integration of their work and personal lives.

Women who face work-related setbacks present unique challenges to coaches as a result of the highly charged emotional intensity of the engagement, and at times, the expectations of key organizational stakeholders. However, coaches can play instrumental roles in helping women overcome these challenges. Coaches who develop an awareness of resiliency-building strategies and skills with key coaching competencies have the ability to coach women to achieve transformational outcomes beyond mere survival.

If you are a people developer, you are now aware of the actions you need to take to effectively coach and mentor women who face work-related challenges. Make a list of the knowledge, competencies, and resiliency strategies you need to focus on to be able to help women thrive and transform, and then take action.

A CALL TO ACTION FOR ORGANIZATIONAL LEADERS

Organizational leaders, through their organizations, play a key role in helping women build the resiliency necessary to overcome work challenges. Organizational leaders play an even more important role in reducing the work challenges that women face that are related to gender discrimination. Women comprise 50 percent of the workforce, and yet based on research by LeanIn.org and McKinsey & Company, programs, policies, and practices have been slow to change. Women continue to encounter challenges at work that cause significant stress, including gender-related issues that men do not face. The call to action for organizational leaders is to (1) remove gender-related roadblocks that cause women challenges at work, and (2) implement programs and practices that help women increase resiliency.

It is good business for organizations to put programs and practices into place to help women build resiliency. Not only are women 50 percent of the workforce, they also make up a large percentage of the consumers of the products and services businesses offer. A research study conducted by Mercer shows that organizations with diverse boards and leadership teams outperform those that are not diverse. By implementing actions that eliminate roadblocks and help women build resiliency, organizations will be able to make more effective use of diverse talent, retain leaders, reduce turnover costs, and increase business results.

REMOVE GENDER-RELATED ROADBLOCKS THAT CAUSE WOMEN CHALLENGES AT WORK

Women experience an uneven playing field at work, due to gender-related issues, and organizations are not perceived as making gender diversity a priority. The following list contains a few important steps an organizational leader can take to remove the roadblocks and ensure that employees and customers see that they have gender diversity as a priority.

- Conduct an organizational audit to identify the roadblocks to resiliency that exist for women. Collect data using surveys, focus groups, and interviews, and engage women in conducting the audit.

- Implement an overarching philosophy about the importance of diversity and a diverse workforce. Establish, track, and monitor the organization's diversity statistics. Hold managers accountable for achieving diversity goals.

- Eliminate discriminatory practices, including harassment, hostile work environments, and bullying, by educating managers and members of the workforce about gender-specific issues. Train employees to recognize discriminatory practices and develop an understanding of how certain behaviors caused by gender bias lead to discrimination. Discrimination consists of ingrained behaviors that can only be changed with a strong stance from leaders at the highest levels in companies.

- Implement a proactive approach to promoting the appropriate values, practices, and policies that will foster employee engagement and allow all employees to use their talents to their full potential. Take immediate action when the values, practices, and policies are violated.

- Ensure that gender bias is eliminated from the organization's hiring practices. Often the list of candidates put forward to fill a position is not diverse and may not include many women. Track and monitor the hiring statistics. Train everyone involved in hiring on how to use unbiased interviewing skills. Make sure that the pool of candidates for a job is diverse and that qualified, diverse candidates are hired.

- Implement a performance management process without gender bias. Performance management is a process that often includes gender biases. Women are often rated lower than men, as gender biases often cause male performance to be rated higher. Train those who evaluate performance on the types of biases that can affect a performance evaluation system.

- Create succession management programs that measure and monitor the progress of women through the leadership pipeline. Succession management programs are an excellent way to track the diversity statistics within an organization and see who is progressing. If the pipeline contains an equal number of men and women, but the leadership ranks are primarily male, then explore what may be causing this blockage.

- Handle business factors such as mergers and downsizing in such a way as to avoid unfair and biased practices. Companies should implement objective performance evaluation processes equitably across the organization at all levels to avoid having women singled out at times of downsizing.

IMPLEMENT PROGRAMS AND PRACTICES THAT HELP WOMEN INCREASE RESILIENCY

Resiliency is the number-one attribute that women need to be successful at work in the 21st century, according to McKinsey & Company. Women need to be able to persevere through challenging circumstances and have a mindset for growth. Essentially, they need to be able to thrive and transform when faced with challenges, not just survive. The following list contains several suggestions on how organizational leaders can help women increase resiliency and thrive. The list represents global best practices and is not all-inclusive.

- Identify internal role models—women who exemplify resiliency— and engage them in championing efforts to help women increase resiliency.

- Implement women's affinity groups. These groups enable women to informally network and provide educational opportunities and conferences on women-related issues. They provide women with a strong sense of support by discussing issues openly that directly relate to women and work.

- Use formal mentoring programs to enable women to build networks required to be successful on the job. Women often believe that if they do their job well, that will be enough. Formal mentoring relationships help women learn how to navigate organizations and develop important job skills. Train mentors, both male and female, on coaching and resiliency strategies.

- Create formal sponsorship relationships between women and leaders who can sponsor their progression through the organization. Sponsors are different from mentors. Sponsors focus on helping women get the necessary job opportunities, visibility, and developmental feedback to move their careers forward. Make sure that sponsors are knowledgeable about the challenges women face at work and what needs to happen to overcome those challenges.

- Establish resiliency as one of the core competencies for your organization. When resiliency is established as a core competency, activities can be aligned to promote development and growth in resiliency.

- Provide resiliency training and education to both women and men in organizations. The six strategies in this book have been proven to help women thrive and transform, to overcome the challenges they face. Resiliency training will also help others in the organization to better mentor and coach women through difficulties.

- Implement work and life balance practices that enable women to reduce the challenges encountered as they try to balance the two often opposing priorities. These practices may include increased maternity leave, flexible work hours, and policies for working remotely. Ensure employees are not afraid to use these practices.

- Provide curricula at universities and colleges that contain education for both women and men related to gender issues at work, including sabotage and building resiliency. Many women who participated in the research for this book felt that they would have been much better equipped to handle the challenges at work if they had known what to expect.

- Create discussion groups about derailment and resiliency in outplacement firms. Outplacement firms provide services to many women who experience career derailment. Unfortunately, these discussions would be reactive versus proactive, but women want a forum in which to share their experiences and need to feel that they are not alone.

Catalyst, a global nonprofit organization that focuses on expanding opportunities for women, has been rewarding companies for best practices in the recruitment, development, and advancement of all women, including diverse women, since 1987. These companies are required to show approaches with proven, measurable results. Below are two examples of award-winning global companies, the programs they implemented, and the results achieved.

- Proctor & Gamble implemented a global initiative with a focus on advancing women across the organization. They provide training, career development, mentorship and sponsorship opportunities.

Also offered are affinity groups, work-life and flexibility programs. Proctor & Gamble achieved excellent results. Between 2008 and 2013, women's representation increased globally from 25.7 percent to 28.3 percent at and above the VP level, from 29.3 percent to 31.8 percent among Associate Directors, and from 40.2 percent to 43.6 percent among all managers. Women's representation on the Board of Directors has increased from 27.3 percent to 50.0 percent. The global retention rate of women employees increased from 87.0 percent to 91.0 percent.

• Kimberly-Clark implemented a global initiative focused on the important role women play in the marketplace and workplace. Goals and activities focus on accelerating the recruitment, development, and retention of women around the world, using succession management and talent pools. Kimberly-Clark achieved excellent results. Between 2009 and 2013, women's representation among Director and above roles has increased globally from 19.0 percent to 26.0 percent; internal promotions of women to Director and above jobs has increased significantly, from 19.0 percent to 44.0 percent. Additionally, women's representation on the Board of Directors has increased from 16.7 percent to 25.0 percent.

These recommendations provided for organizational leaders, if implemented in organizations, will help move the topic of women's career challenges and resiliency into an informed space that will enable women to better manage their careers. Also, organizations will be able to effectively recruit, develop, promote, and retain a talented workforce of women to help grow the business and increase results. If you work in an organization, you are now aware. List the actions you will take immediately to help women overcome work-related challenges, and thrive.

A CALL TO ACTION FOR MEN

Men play a unique role in supporting women in their efforts to enhance their resiliency and achieve greater success. Men can provide support at home by helping their wives and partners build resiliency. In many organizations, men have greater access to power and resources than women and can share those resources to help women build resiliency. The list below includes important actions that men can take to support women and help build their resiliency.

- Get educated about women's issues. Learn about the unique challenges and dilemmas that women face in the workplace. Ask female colleagues about their experiences. Chapter 1 in this book is an excellent starting point.

- Make yourself available to support women, both on and off the job. Women may not proactively approach men for support and guidance. Be explicit about communicating your willingness to perform this role. Find opportunities to communicate your commitment to supporting the growth of women.

- Look for opportunities to champion women. If you are in a leadership role, find ways to work on behalf of women getting recognition for their accomplishments, visible work assignments, and access to other key leaders.

- Become a sponsor or a mentor of a woman. Create an ongoing supportive relationship with emerging women leaders, either individually or in groups. Some organizations have affinity networking groups for women. If your organization does, consider being a sponsor or regular speaker.

- Challenge the status quo with your male counterparts. Challenge your male colleagues when they base their hiring, promotion, or work assignments on outdated assumptions and gender stereotypes.

- Provide developmental feedback to women. Find ways to provide critical developmental feedback to emerging women leaders.

- Draw women into strategic conversations. Find ways to engage women in strategic conversations to help them build awareness of how these conversations happen and enhance their visibility.

- Provide stretch assignments, particularly in line operations. Find ways to engage women on assignments associated with line operations so they can develop vital skills and visibility.

- Use the tools and resources in this book to build your own resiliency. It will help you to learn the resiliency strategies and develop your own resilience-building actions. You will be in a better position to help women by speaking from your own experience in applying these tools and strategies.

As you support women and look for ways to help them build their resiliency, work within your own sphere of influence. Although you may not be able to change cultures, you can strongly influence the culture in your own home or organization. Become a role model in your personal and professional life by tapping into the unique strengths that women demonstrate. As a man, you are now aware of the actions you can take to help women build their resiliency. Make a list of the actions that you will take to show support.

Women, people developers, organizational leaders, and men need to take action now. This book and the suggestions provided will help women build resiliency, and not just survive workplace challenges, but thrive and grow. By making a conscious choice and taking these actions, women can transform their lives and achieve the career satisfaction they deserve.

READER'S GUIDE

Discussion Questions: These questions can be used as discussion questions for book clubs and other reading groups, as well as for individual reflection.

Chapter 1: Navigating Career Adversity

1. To what extent have you had an experience like Oprah where a career setback turned out to be a blessing?

2. Which of the four career derailment sources (personal factors, other individuals, organizational, societal) have you experienced or observed in other women?

3. In what ways has your resiliency helped you navigate some of the challenges you have faced in your career?

4. Which of the three case vignettes (Maria, Barbara or Yolanda) do you most identify with?

Chapter 2: Laying the Foundation

1. Reflect on a significant roadblock you faced in your career. Which of the six strategies were most critical in your ability to regain your resiliency?

2. Which of the six strategies would you consider to be your strongest? Which of the six strategies are your most vulnerable?

3. What might be the impact on your career if you focus on the resiliency strategy with which you feel most vulnerable?

4. Who do you think you could tap to assemble a support group to build your resiliency?

Chapters 3, 5, 7, 9, 11, and 13: The Women's Personal Resiliency Stories

1. Which woman's story did you personally relate to? What about the story resonated with you?

2. Have you, or someone you know, experienced bullying at work? How can someone build resiliency and thrive in the face of bullying on-the-job?

3. These women made significant changes in their careers in order to achieve the life they desired. What were the key resiliency strategies they used to make these changes? What actions did they take that you will implement?

4. What is the most important idea you took away from the six personal resiliency stories? How will you use what you have learned?

Chapter 4: Strengthen Support Networks

1. Which aspects of Marti's story links to your experiences navigating tough times in your career?

2. As you reflect on your career and challenges you faced, who played a significant role in helping you regain your footing? In what ways did this person help you?

3. To what extent do any of the derailment triggers resonate for you at this point in your career?

4. Chapter 4 describes how Kelsey Ramsden used a "reinvention mentor" to help her make a major transition in her career. As you reflect on your career and transitions you have made, who served as your reinvention mentor?

Chapter 6: Clarify Purpose

1. Which of the derailment triggers in Jane's story have you experienced?

2. What are your core values and how to they shape the kind of work that you do?

3. What actions will you take to increase your satisfaction with two of your passions and interests identified on the Passions and Interests Life Wheel?

4. Are you doing work that is aligned with the vision you have for your career? If yes, how have you achieved that alignment? If no, what are your next steps to get better alignment between your vision and the work you do?

Chapter 8: Build Self-Awareness

1. What does the following quote by Lynn Schmidt mean to you? "When someone holds the mirror up, stop to take a look. Be open to the gift of self-awareness."

2. As Francesca found out, identifying development needs isn't always easy. How can you identify unconscious development needs in order to grow and increase your resiliency?

3. Billy Jean King has been quoted as saying "I think self-awareness is probably the most important thing towards being a champion." Why is self-awareness so important for success?

4. How do you identify and control your emotional hot buttons? What is the most useful technique that you use to make conscious choices about your reactions to others?

Chapter 10: Enhance Self-Care

1. Lynn Schmidt states "Building resiliency is all about getting uncomfortable." How does accomplishing goals outside of your comfort zone make you stronger?

2. Elaina experienced significant stress in her new role. When have you experienced job related stress and how did you overcome it?

3. In order to enhance your self-care, you need to be focused on physical, emotional, and spiritual well-being. Which one is most important for you to focus on right now and how will you increase your well-being?

4. Arianna Huffington's story is a good example of what happens when you don't practice self-care. How can you avoid sacrificing your professional success in order to achieve inner peace?

Chapter 12: Actualize Strengths

1. Lin experienced some significant challenges along her journey to becoming self-employed and in retrospect may not have been a good fit for entrepreneurship. To what extent have you considered self-employment? How well would self-employment fit your personality?

2. If you found yourself in an elevator with a notable in your profession, what are three of your strengths you would want to communicate to this person?

3. Reflect on a peak experience in your career history. In what ways did it tap your biggest strengths?

4. When do you feel most powerful in your career? What are the conditions or factors that contribute to your awareness of your power?

Chapter 14: Broaden Coping Skills

1. Reflect on a career challenge you faced. How well did you cope with it? In retrospect, what would you do differently?

2. Have you ever experienced or witnessed sabotage in the workplace? What did it teach you about navigating career adversity?

3. What strategies do you use to work through your emotions when you face tough times?

4. To what extent do you embrace a growth perspective in your personal and professional lives? What kinds of self-talk do you use when you are holding a growth-oriented mindset?

Chapter 15: A Call To Action

1. Which of the suggestions for how women can support other women do you think are most important? How do you plan to support other women?

2. Has a coach or mentor played a pivotal role in helping you build your resiliency? What did the coach or mentor do that was so helpful?

3. How can organizations remove gender-related roadblocks that cause women challenges at work?

4. What actions would you like to see the men in your life (father, brother, partner, manager, or friend) take to support women and help build their resiliency?

ACKNOWLEDGMENTS

The multi-year journey to write this book would have been insurmountable without the generosity and support of so many people.

Numerous coaches provided us with their wisdom and insights on how women thrive when faced with difficult challenges. Thank you to all of the coaches we talked with, and a special note of thanks to the coaches we initially interviewed who bring a passion to this work that provided the foundation for our research. Micki Berg, Ken Buch, Julie Francisco, Steve Heller, Kelly Kienzle, Tom Lombardi, Rebekah Lowe, Melanie Polk, Jenn Sellers, Anne Teehan, and Christopher Weber-Furst, we greatly appreciate your contributions to this book. For those coaches that expressed interest we have listed brief biographies at the end of these acknowledgements.

Several women shared inspiring stories of hope and resiliency as a part of our research process. While we are not sharing their names as we committed to preserving their anonymity, they embody the spirit of resiliency. Thank you for your support of our book and of women everywhere. We wish you all the best as you move forward in your careers.

A manuscript needs beta readers to help it become a book that will be useful and appealing to the target audiences. The feedback we received from those that read the first drafts of our manuscript was immensely helpful. Thank you to the colleagues and friends, Lisa Jetland Alexander, Holly Burkett, Pam Coffey, Toni DeTuncq, Katherine Handin, Patrice Henning, Connie Karlsson, Dan McLinden, Lynn Myhal, and Brian Scott who served as beta readers for our manuscript. A special note of thanks to the many family members who provided informal input to our work as it moved forward. To our editor Frank Steele and designer Matt Bright, your patience and amazing talents were such a gift during the production process.

Six women contributed their personal short stories of resiliency to this book. Their narratives are both inspiring and motivating. It took courage to share their transformation with the world. Each of their stories adds a deeper dimension to the book and illustrates what a difficult journey building resiliency can be. Their stories demonstrate how building resiliency contributed to their success, satisfaction, and happiness. Thank you to Francoise Evenou, Linda Fullman, Marianne Rauturier, Anna Steffeney, Sandy Swanton, and Ruchika Tulshyan for your contributions and encouragement. We wish you continued success are you use your resiliency strategies to create the lives you desire and serve as role models to women around the globe.

Several professional organizations supported our work while it was in development. We were invited to make presentations and write articles about women, work, and resiliency for these organizations: American Speech-Language-Hearing Association, Association of Talent Development, CoachSource, Fielding Graduate University, International Coach Federation, InterNations, and the Professional Women's Network Global. Thank you for your ongoing support. A special note of thanks to Joel Digirolamo, Director of Coaching Science with the International Coach Federation, for supporting our work and allowing us to tap the wisdom of several hundred International Coach Federation members.

There have been hundreds of people who have provided input along the way as part of informal discussions. Thank you to all the people, men and women alike, who provided suggestions and demonstrated excitement about this topic. Everyone we talked with expressed how important a focus on women, work, and resiliency is to individuals and organizations. We are looking forward to continuing these discussions as we work to help women everywhere build resiliency and experience the careers they desire and deserve.

Coaches' Biographies

Ken Buch, PCC, MSOD
Location: Washington, DC, USA
Email: Ken@shift-tcc.com or kgbuch@gmail.com
Phone: 240-277-3452
Description: Founder, Ken Buch of SHIFT Transformational Coaching and Consulting, LLC a boutique firm, offers custom solutions to meet clients' needs. Mr. Buch earned his coach certification at Georgetown University, a PCC designation through the International Coach Federation, a Post Graduate Certification in the Neuroscience of Leadership from Middlesex University, UK, and an MBSLA certification through ABL. Ken is a Fellow in Change Management and holds an M.S. in Organizational Development from Johns Hopkins University.

Steve Heller
Location: Lorton, VA, USA (suburb of Washington, DC)
Website: www.hellercoaching.com
Email: steve@hellercoaching.com
Phone: 703-646-5507
Description: Leadership coach, currently focused on work with leaders of social enterprises.

Kelly Kienzle
Location: Charlottesville, VA, USA
Website: www.opencirclecoaching.com
Email: kelly@opencirclecoaching.com
Phone: 202-841-0702
Description: Open Circle Coaching provides leadership coaching, workshop facilitation, 360-degree interviews and leadership development programs. We partner with organizations that are committed to broadening the perspectives of their existing leaders and building the capabilities of their next generation of leaders. Our clients adopt new mindsets and learn effective tools to bring about greater organizational and individual success.

Rebekah M. Lowe, CLC ACC
Location: Asheville, NC, USA
Website: FizzyWork.com
Email: Rlowe@fizzywork.com
Phone: 828-215-8781
Description: FizzyWork Executive Coaching strives to help work become "Fizzy": fulfilling, engaging, and rewarding, to create passionate leaders who exceed performance targets, joyfully. We serve leaders and their teams nationwide, through coaching of individual leaders, group and team coaching, workshops and training seminars, and keynote addresses. We believe in work at its best, for leaders who are effervescent.

Alexis Williamson
Location: Victoria, British Columbia CANADA
Website: Executivecoachbc.ca
Email: alexisw@shaw.ca
Phone: 250-514-6934
Description: Multidisciplinary Executive and Leadership coaching with internal organizational and external public and private sector organizations – with a specific focus on women in the workplace.

NOTES

CHAPTER 1

Oprah's failures: Julie Zeilinger, "7 Influential Women Who Failed Before They Succeeded," *The Huffington Post*, July 24, 2013, http://www.huffingtonpost.com/2013/07/24/7-women-who-failed-before-they-succeeded_n_3640835.html.

Oprah's life chronology: Academy of Achievement, "Oprah Winfrey Biography," last modified August 31, 2015, http://www.achievement.org/autodoc/page/win0bio-1.

Oprah's demotion from WJZ-TV: Jane Marion, "When Oprah Was Ours," *Baltimore*, May 2011, http://www.baltimoremagazine.net/2011/5/when-oprah-was-ours.

Quote from Oprah: Oprah Winfrey, *What I Know For Sure* (New York: Flatiron Books, 2014), 45.

Oprah's interview with David Letterman: Jenny Johnson, "Oprah: I was raped when I was only 9," *Irish Examiner*, November 28, 2012, http://www.irishexaminer.com/world/oprah-i-was-raped-when-i-was-only-9-215310.html.

Mercer report on representation of women in the workforce: Mercer, "When Women Thrive, Businesses Thrive," 2014, http://www.mercer.com/insights/point/2014/when-women-thrive-businesses-thrive-PDF.html.

Women as entrepreneurs: Emily Fetsch, Chris Jackson, and Jason Wiens, "Women Entrepreneurs Are Key to Accelerating Growth," *Entrepreneurship Policy Digest*, July 20, 2015, http://www.kauffman.org/~/media/kauffman_org/resources/2015/entrepreneurship%20policy%20digest/july%202015/women_entrepreneurs_are_key_to_accelerating_growth.pdf.

Gender diversity and performance: Vivian Hunt, Dennis Layton, and Sara Prince, "Why Diversity Matters," McKinsey & Company, January

2015, http://www.mckinsey.com/insights/organization/why_diversity_
matters.

**Female board members and improved corporate performance in
Sweden:** Charlotte Clarke, "Research shows profitable companies have
more women on the board," *Financial Times*, July 25, 2013, http://
www.ft.com/intl/cms/s/2/2d320562-f52d-11e2-94e9-00144feabdc0.
html#axzz3xboETd00.

Global impact of improving women's equality: Jonathan Woetzel et
al., "How advancing women's equality can add $12 trillion to global
growth," McKinsey Global Institute, September 2015, http://www.
mckinsey.com/insights/growth/how_advancing_womens_equality_
can_add_12_trillion_to_global_growth.

Closing the wage gap: Oliver Cann, "It's Back to the Future as Women's
Pay Finally Equals Men's ... From 2006," World Economic Forum,
2015, http://reports.weforum.org/global-gender-gap-report-2015/
press-releases/.

Gender parity research: Julie Coffman and Bill Neuenfeldt, "Everyday
moments of truth: Frontline managers are key to women's career
aspirations," Bain & Company, July 17, 2014, http://www.bain.com/
publications/articles/everyday-moments-of-truth.aspx.

Department of Labor Statistics: "Futurework—Trends and Challenges
for Work in the 21st Century: Executive Summary," 1999, United States
Department of Labor, http://www.dol.gov/oasam/programs/history/
herman/reports/futurework/
execsum.htm.

Missing rights: Emily Crockett, "This UN report shows that women's
rights in the US are an international embarrassment," *Vox* Identities,
December 18, 2015,
http://www.vox.com/2015/12/18/10587126/un-womens-rights-
embarrassment.

2012 statistics on women in the C-Suite: "A CEO's guide to gender
equality," *McKinsey Quarterly*, November 2015, http://www.mckinsey.
com/insights/
leading_in_the_21st_century/a_ceos_guide_to_gender_equality.

UN study on women in government: "Facts and Figures: Leadership
and Political Participation," UN Women, updated January 2016,

http://www.unwomen.org/en/what-we-do/leadership-and-political-participation/facts-and-figures.

Recent statistics in the United States: Anna Brown, "The Data on Women Leaders," Pew Research Center, January 14, 2015, http://www.pewsocialtrends.org/2015/01/14/the-data-on-women-leaders/.

Recent global statistics: "2014 Catalyst Census: Women Board Directors," Catalyst Research, January 13, 2015, http://www.catalyst.org/knowledge/2014-catalyst-census-women-board-directors.

Discrimination statistics: "Futurework—Trends and Challenges for Work in the 21st Century: Executive Summary," 1999, United States Department of Labor, http://www.dol.gov/oasam/programs/history/herman/reports/futurework/execsum.htm.

Stereotypes: Madeline E. Heilman, "Gender stereotypes and workplace bias," *Research in Organizational Behavior* 32 (2012): 117, http://www.academia.edu/7976875/Gender_stereotypes_and_workplace_bias.

Recent statistics in the United States: Anna Brown, "The Data on Women Leaders," Pew Research Center, January 14, 2015, http://www.pewsocialtrends.org/2015/01/14/the-data-on-women-leaders/.

HBR study: "Women in the Workplace: A Research Roundup," *Harvard Business Review*, September 2013, 86–89, https://hbr.org/2013/09/women-in-the-workplace-a-research-roundup.

Important qualities for women's success: Lareina Yee, "Fostering women leaders: A fitness test for your top team," *McKinsey Quarterly*, January 2015, http://www.mckinsey.com/insights/organization/fostering_women_leaders_a_fitness_test_for_your_top_team.

Factors contributing to women's success in developing countries: Anita Newton, "The No. 1 Trait of Successful Women Entrepreneurs Around the World," *Inc.*, March 6, 2015, http://www.inc.com/anita-newton/the-no-1-trait-of-successful-women-entrepreneurs-around-the-world.html.

Rate of derailment and organizational costs: Joyce Hogan, Robert Hogan, and Robert Kaiser, "Management Derailment: Personality Assessment and Mitigation" in *APA Handbook of Industrial and Organizational Psychology*, edited by Sheldon Zedeck (Washington, DC: American Psychological Association, 2010).

Derailment sources for women: Lynn Schmidt, *Executive Women's Perceptions of Their Career Derailment* (BiblioBazaar, 2011).

CHAPTER 2

Research on writing down goals: "Dominican Research Cited in Forbes Article," Dominican University, http://www.dominican.edu/dominicannews/dominican-research-cited-in-forbes-article.

Social support: Sidney Cobb, "Social support as a moderator of life stress," *Psychosomatic Medicine* 38, no. 5 (1976): 300–314.

Optimism: Martin E. P. Seligman, *Learned Optimism* (New York: Free Press, 1990).

Positive emotions: Barbara Fredrickson, *Positivity* (New York: Crown, 2009).

Physical resiliency: David Hellerstein, "How Can I Become More Resilient?" *Psychology Today*, August 27, 2011, https://www.psychologytoday.com/blog/heal-your-brain/201108/how-can-i-become-more-resilient.

Spiritual resiliency in the US Air Force: "Spiritual Resilience," United States Air Force, http://www.sheppard.af.mil/shared/media/document/AFD-130325-058.pdf.

Emotional regulation: Allison S. Troy and Iris B. Mauss, "Resilience in the face of stress: emotion regulation as a protective factor," in S.M. Southwick, B.T. Litz, D. Charney, and M.J. Friedman, eds., *Resilience and Mental Health: Challenges Across the Lifespan* (Boston, MA: Cambridge University Press, 2011), 30–44.

Self-efficacy: Albert Bandura, *Self-Efficacy: The exercise of control* (New York: W.H. Freeman, 1997).

CHAPTER 4

Kelsey Ramsden: Eric Wagner, "8 Simple Tips From A $50M Female Entrepreneur," *Forbes*, February 4, 2014, http://www.forbes.com/sites/ericwagner/2014/02/04/8-simple-tips-from-a-50-million-female-entrepreneur/.

Kelsey Ramsden Blog: Kelsey Ramsden, "How to Reinvent Yourself," *Entrepreneur*, February 6, 2015, http://www.entrepreneur.com/article/241593.

Ramsden's cancer: Sean Meyer, "Run for Ovarian Cancer," *Our London*, May 14, 2012, http://www.londoncommunitynews.com/community-story/1357858-run-for-ovarian-cancer/.

Ramsden on networking: Kelsey Ramsden, "Making Connections vs. Maintaining Connections: Which Is Worth More?" *The Huffington Post*, June 18, 2014, http://www.huffingtonpost.ca/kelsey-ramsden/making-maintaining-connections_b_5507379.html.

CHAPTER 6

Mika Brzezinski's Story: Mika Brzezinski, "The Road Not Taken: How Getting Fired Boosted My Career," *LinkedIn Pulse*, November 17, 2014, https://www.linkedin.com/pulse/20141117231227-345816243-the-road-not-taken-how-getting-fired-boosted-my-career?trk=prof-post.

CHAPTER 8

Billie Jean King's Story: Tim Ott, "Billie Jean King Biography," biography.com, accessed January 16, 2016, http://www.biography.com/people/billie-jean-king-9364876.

Billie Jean King Interview: Jessica Hopper, "Always Starting Over: An Interview with Billie Jean King," *Rookie*, October 14, 2013, http://www.rookiemag.com/2013/10/billie-jean-king/.

Stages of competence: Linda Adams, "Learning a New Skill is Easier Said Than Done," Gordon Training International, accessed January 17, 2016,
http://www.gordontraining.com/free-workplace-articles/learning-a-new-skill-is-easier-said-than-done/.

CHAPTER 10

Arianna Huffington's Story: Adam Grant, "Arianna Huffington on How to Thrive," Knowledge@Wharton, April 11, 2014, http://knowledge.wharton.upenn.edu/article/third-metric-success-arianna-huffington/.

CHAPTER 12

Sal's Shoes: CJ Bowry, "Our Story," Sal's Shoes, http://www.salsshoes.com/our-story/.

Camilla Bowry's background: Camila Bowry, personal interview conducted with the author, September 30, 2015.

CHAPTER 14
Growth mindset: Carol Dweck, *Mindset: The New Psychology of Success* (New York: Ballantine Books, 2006).
Malala's story: Malala Yousafzai and Christina Lamb, *I Am Malala: The girl who stood up for education and was shot by the Taliban* (New York: Little, Brown and Company, 2013).

CHAPTER 15
Lean In and McKinsey report on women in the workplace: LeanIn. org and McKinsey & Company, *Women in the Workplace* (2015), http://womenintheworkplace.com/.
Mercer report on women and businesses: Mercer, "When Women Thrive, Businesses Thrive," 2014, http://www.mercer.com/insights/point/2014/when-women-thrive-businesses-thrive-PDF.html.
Resiliency is the number-one attribute: Lareina Yee, "Fostering Women Leaders: A Fitness Test for Your Top Team," *McKinsey Quarterly*, January 2015, http://www.mckinsey.com/insights/organization/fostering_women_leaders_a_fitness_test_for_your_top_team.
Catalyst award winners: Catalyst, "Catalyst 20th Anniversary Award Compendium," Catalyst Award Winners, accessed January 16, 2016, http://www.catalyst.org/catalyst-award-winners.

AUTHORS' BIOGRAPHIES

Lynn Schmidt, PhD

Dr. Lynn Schmidt is a global talent management and organization development leader who has a passion for helping women successfully navigate and avoid career setbacks. Her passion for helping women developed during her more than twenty years of experience working in Fortune 500 companies. Lynn observed women facing unusual career setbacks, and as she climbed the corporate ladder she experienced her own career derailment challenges. She has focused her career on the areas of talent management that she believes can be most helpful to women in the workplace, including succession management, leadership development, career development, mentoring, diversity, and coaching programs. While writing this book, Lynn took a one-year sabbatical to focus on her own resiliency building.

Lynn is an executive coach with over fifteen years of global experience coaching executive, mid-level, and frontline leaders. She received her Evidence Based Coaching Certification from Fielding Graduate University and earned her Associate Certified Coach (ACC) credential. Her decision to further develop her skills as an executive coach was directly tied to her passion for helping women leaders achieve the careers they deserve. Lynn received the Talent Leadership Award at the World HRD Congress in Mumbai, India, for her contributions to the field of talent development.

Lynn earned her PhD in 2009. Her dissertation research focused on executive women's perspectives of the factors that had contributed to their career derailment. She interviewed more than two dozen female executives and created a framework that illustrated the four components of career derailment for women. Lynn is the author, co-author, chapter author and editor of several publications focused on improving workplace learning, leadership development, and talent management, including *Integrated Talent Management Scorecards:*

Insights from World-Class Organizations on Demonstrating Value (DeTuncq & Schmidt, 2013, ASTD Press).

Lynn is a frequent keynote speaker and presenter at conferences in North America, South America, Europe, and Asia. She presents on a variety of topics, such as resiliency, women and career derailment, integrated talent management, leadership development, succession management, and training scorecards. Lynn participates in several professional organizations, including the International Coach Federation, Association for Talent Development, Society for Human Resource Management, InterNations, and the Global Professional Women's Network.

She contributes to a variety of social network sites, including Facebook (www.facebook.comLynnSchmidtAuthor), LinkedIn (https://www.linkedin.com/in/lynnschmidt), and Twitter (@LM_Schmidt). You can contact her at lschmidt912@hotmail.com and visit her website at www.schmidtleadership.com.

KEVIN NOURSE, PhD, PCC

Dr. Kevin Nourse is an executive coach, leadership researcher, speaker, and adjunct professor with a passion for helping leaders and managers resiliently navigate change and adversity. Kevin identified his commitment to helping people develop resiliency when his mother developed lung cancer in 1995. After her death, he immersed himself in the hospice movement as a volunteer with ten patients facing terminal diseases. Despite their imminent death, many of these patients shared hope-filled stories about their lives and legacies. This experience introduced Kevin to the concept of resiliency and the power of intentionally choosing one's attitude toward adversity.

Kevin has significant experience working with individuals facing career adversity, as well as his own experience navigating career derailment. In his role as a human resource director at PricewaterhouseCoopers Consulting, he launched a career management center to help staff enhance their career resilience. When faced with an organizational downsizing at PwC, Kevin volunteered to give up his job, start his own firm, and practice what he preached about reframing adversity to workshop participants. He initially focused his coaching practice on helping over 200 people who had been downsized find new jobs. This experience deepened his knowledge and practical experience helping people sustain and enhance their resiliency.

Currently, he serves as an executive coach and facilitator, supporting the development of women leaders, particularly in healthcare professions. Three of his major clients are professional associations where the majority of members are women. Kevin designed and facilitates a comprehensive yearlong leadership development academy for members of these organizations who aspire to be leaders. A portion of the curriculum focuses on enhancing career resiliency.

In addition to his practical experience with women leaders and resiliency, he brings a strong research background to his work. Kevin earned a PhD in 2009 based on his research about resilient leadership during Hurricane Katrina in New Orleans. Kevin conducted another study in 2010 that involved interviews with 15 CEOs of port authorities in the United States and Canada. This study focused on understanding how these leaders coped with and responded to the 2009 global economic crisis. His research specifically explored how leaders use strategic thinking skills and practices to resiliently thrive in the face of crisis.

Kevin writes a blog entitled The Leaders' Advocate that explores contemporary issues faced by leaders in their development. He is a certified professional coach and faculty member at Georgetown University. Kevin is a member of the American College of Healthcare Executives (ACHE), American Psychological Association (APA), American Society for Healthcare Human Resources Administration (ASHHRA), International Coach Federation (ICF), International Leadership Association (ILA), and the International Positive Psychology Association (IPPA). In 2001 he founded Nourse Leadership Strategies (www.nourseleadership.com), a Washington, DC, and Los Angeles-based professional services firm offering executive coaching, team coaching and development, and leadership development programs. Kevin can be reached at kevin@nourseleadership.com and Twitter (@drkevinnourse).

CPSIA information can be obtained
at www.ICGtesting.com
Printed in the USA
LVOW11s1555160917

548593LV00002B/22/P